C000007463

# ARSENAL

## THE CHAMPIONS' YEAR

### THE INSIDE STORY OF
### THE GUNNERS' 1989—90 SEASON

*Also by Harry Miller (with David O'Leary)*
My Story

# ARSENAL

## THE CHAMPIONS' YEAR

### THE INSIDE STORY OF THE GUNNERS' 1989—90 SEASON

—————BY—————

## THE ARSENAL 1st TEAM SQUAD
## WITH HARRY MILLER

PARTRIDGE PRESS

LONDON · NEW YORK · TORONTO · SYDNEY · AUCKLAND

To the chairman, staff and players of Arsenal Football Club,
for telling it as it happened. And to Ina, for her support
and encouragement.

TRANSWORLD PUBLISHERS LTD
61–63 Uxbridge Road, London W5 5SA

TRANSWORLD PUBLISHERS (AUSTRALIA)
PTY LTD
15–23 Helles Avenue, Moorebank, NSW 2170

TRANSWORLD PUBLISHERS (NZ) LTD
Cnr Moselle and Waipareira Aves,
Henderson, Auckland

Published 1990 by Partridge Press
a division of Transworld Publishers Ltd
Copyright © 1990 Jerome Anderson Management
Limited

The right of Harry Miller to be identified
as author of this work has been asserted in
accordance with sections 77 and 78 of the Copyright
Designs and Patents Act 1988.

British Library Catalogue in Publication Data
Arsenal : the champion's year : the inside story of
the Gunners' 1989–90 season.
1. England. Association football. Clubs.
Arsenal Football Club
I. Miller, Harry 1938–   II. Arsenal Football Club
796.334630942143

ISBN 1–85225–122–0

All rights reserved. No part of this publication may
be reproduced, stored in a retrieval system, or
transmitted in any form or by any means,
electronic, mechanical, photocopying, recording,
or otherwise, without the prior permission of
the publishers.

Typeset by Photoprint, Torquay, Devon
Printed in Great Britain
by Richard Clay PLC, Bungay

The publishers wish to thank Jerome Anderson
Management, the exclusive representatives of the
Arsenal players pool, for getting this project off
the ground and for all their subsequent help and
co-operation.

Cover and book design by Lee Griffiths.

Photographs courtesy of: **Action Images** pp.6, 9, 10,
14, 16, 21, 22, 24, 25, 27, 28, 30, 33, 40, 49, 52, 54, 65,
70, 72, 76, 83, 90, 91, 100, 107, 110, 113; **Allsport**
p.19/Simon Bruty pp.36, 123, 129/David Cannon
pp.67, 146/Roger Labrosse pp.50, 96/Christine Lalla
p.104/Bob Martin p.140/Gray Mortimore p.102/Nick
Potts pp.56, 89, 150/Ben Radford pp.46, 116/Chris
Raphael pp.38, 148/Dan Smith pp.12, 61, 86, 92, 132;
**Bob Thomas Sports Photography** pp.43, 62, 94,
99, 118, 120, 122, 124, 126, 133, 136, 138, 141, 142,
151, 152; **The Press Association Ltd** pp.45, 58, 69,
115, 131, 134, 144, 154; **The Mail on Sunday** pp.35,
48; **Doug Poole** p.78; **Jerry Munson** p.80; **Bill
Smith** p.84.

# CONTENTS

# 1
# BACK TO WORK

*Brian Marwood*

Brian Marwood went back to work on 13 July 1989, with an appetite sharpened by disappointment. When Arsenal won the most dramatic League championship of modern times, on an unforgettable evening at Anfield the previous May, injury had made him a spectator. Marwood, the quick and brave little winger who reminded older Arsenal fans so much of 70s hero George Armstrong, missed the last five matches of the season following an achilles tendon operation. He still remembers how crowded the team bus was on the night Arsenal went to Liverpool and triumphed against the odds.

'Stewart Houston, the reserve team coach, was there. So was Pat Rice, who looks after the youth side, and Steve Burtenshaw, the chief

◀ **Brian Marwood – a left foot as good as any in the business.**

scout. The lack of tension was quite surprising. But there were the little things that annoyed me at the time. Like getting off the bus at the ground and not knowing where to go. People like Paul Davis and Niall Quinn actually had to sit behind the goal. I would have been shepherded that way too, but I managed to find a spot in the dug-out. It disappointed me that those lads, who had played an important part in what we had achieved, found themselves shoved into the shadows. For me, it was nice to be with the team, nice to be there, nice to experience all the emotions of the evening. But I knew there was a gap. I wasn't actually involved and I know Paul and Niall felt the same way.'

The 1–0 win over Newcastle on 15 April had been Marwood's last game of that marvellous season. In some ways he was lucky. His achilles was not torn. It only needed scraping and he wasn't even in plaster when he accompanied Arsenal to their date with destiny.

'At the final whistle I couldn't resist going on the pitch to join the celebrations. At the back of my mind was the nagging feeling that I shouldn't be doing this. I could be back in hospital the following day. But then I thought . . . to hell with it. This may never ever happen again. Despite my own personal disappointment, I was determined to enjoy every moment.'

Physiotherapist Gary Lewin had told Marwood he would need to work hard throughout the summer to be ready for the new season. Even on holiday in Minorca, Marwood trained every day. 'I didn't mind. I accepted that for me the short break was going to be a hard, hard slog.'

Arsenal, since George Graham became manager, have always reported back at the start of a season to Trent Park, a big open expanse at Cockfosters in Hertfordshire. 'That first day is a catching-up process of what has been happening during the weeks we have been away,' says Marwood. Everyone looks well and much of the talk is about holidays. Portugal seemed to have been a bit of a favourite sun-spot. The skipper –

Tony Adams, Kevin Richardson and Paul Merson were among those who went to the Algarve.

'We had expected the manager to add to the squad. But the only new faces were a dozen youth training scheme kids. We were joking, "The boss is going to introduce his new signings – The Invisible Man, Lord Lucan and Shergar." All professionals are written to in the summer telling them the date they must report back and where to report. At Arsenal, you are also given a weight. You are allowed to be 4lb over, no more. Otherwise, it is a fine of £1 per pound.' There were no fines that first day.

The disciplinary structure at Arsenal also includes a £10 fine if a player is late for training. But he gets two lives. And if he doesn't pay, it is 10 per cent of his wages. The money goes to charity. Being booked for dissent hits the hardest. A first offence is 10 per cent of basic wages – whether you are an international star or the rawest apprentice. A second offence is 20 per cent. Not many players at Highbury make the same mistake a third time!

George Graham's first day team talk was brief and blunt. He told his squad: 'Winning the championship is now history. We are starting all over again. And we want to finish with another trophy.' Tony Adams, Alan Smith, David Rocastle, David O'Leary and Niall Quinn missed manager Graham's battle orders. Because of international duty, they had been given an extra week off. They returned the following Thursday – 24 hours before the squad left to train and play in Sweden. Fifteen players made the trip to Scandinavia – the recognized regulars, the accepted fringe men and two young professionals, goalkeeper Alan Miller and striker Kevin Campbell.

Footballers, when they go away, always share rooms. At Arsenal, goalkeeper John Lukic was the exception. He always had a room on his own. That's the way it was in Sweden. The pairings are based on friendships and similar interests. In the Arsenal camp, Marwood and right back Lee Dixon always double up. 'We signed for the club not long after each other. Our wives get on well and we have become very good friends,' says Marwood. When Martin Hayes was in the squad, he always shared with Adams. They both come from Essex and they grew up at Arsenal together. Nigel Winterburn and Kevin Richardson were inseparable. Winterburn actually bought his house from Richardson. 'We can't work out whether Nigel or Kevin got the better deal,' says Marwood. David O'Leary and Alan Smith share. David Rocastle teams up with Michael Thomas, Paul Merson with Steve Bould and Paul Davis with Gus Caesar.

'A pre-season tour is totally different from going away at the end of the season,' says Marwood. 'There are curfews and everyone knows they have to work. There are no boozy nights out. Even so, you have to be very careful. A *Sun* reporter from the Yorkshire area, Michael Morgan, was in Sweden to cover our games. John Lukic and I knew him and we told the boss and the other players. It was nothing against Michael. The last thing you need, before the season even starts, is the wrong sort of headlines in the tabloid Press.

'It was all pretty hectic. The days seemed to be crammed with coach journeys and moving from hotel to hotel. When we weren't training, we were playing. For one game, we flew to the north of Sweden, had a 2-hour coach journey into Norway, stayed overnight, and did the return journey the following morning. Any spare time I had was spent on Professional Footballers' Association work. At that time, we were sorting out a new bonus scheme at the club. As the union representative, much of the research in putting together an acceptable package fell on me.

'I knew I needed match fitness. The boss was playing me in half a game, then taking me off.

▶ **Marwood, ready to show the world Arsenal were not one-season wonders.**

It was very frustrating. I had worked hard during the summer break and I still wasn't 100 per cent. I felt very depressed. When we got back from Sweden, it was straight into a four-club tournament, in which Liverpool were also involved, at Wembley. We beat Porto 1–0 on the Saturday and Liverpool 1–0 the following day. I didn't play in either game. I wasn't fit. And I was beginning to feel a bit of an outsider. The rest of the squad had the Monday and Tuesday off before flying to Miami for the challenge match that had been arranged the coming Sunday against Independiente of Argentina. I didn't go. I was kept behind to play three matches in the reserves.

'At the time, it felt like a huge kick in the teeth. In fact, it was the best thing that could have happened. I got down to some serious work. Stewart Houston, Arsenal's second team coach, was a tremendous help. I was feeling very low, but he got me involved in what he was doing. It was the lift I needed. There were games at Bishops Stortford, Aylesbury and Margate. I played in all three. So did Paul Davis. He was going through torment. He couldn't understand why, after all the doctors he had seen, all the treatment, all the rest, he was still in pain with his thigh.'

On Sunday, 6 August, Arsenal's first team beat Independiente in Miami and flew home the following day. Assistant manager Theo Foley went from the airport to his home to unpack, then drove down to Margate to watch the reserves.

'He didn't have bags under his eyes. He had suitcases,' said Marwood. 'It was my best game of the three. I scored twice, I felt sharp, I felt fit. Stewart Houston was there. So was Steve Burtenshaw. It meant the boss had three opinions to go on. For all that, I didn't expect to play against Liverpool in the Charity Shield. We were playing five across the back and that was obviously going to limit the scope for me

◁ **Travelling in style – as a champion should.**

11

⬛ **Honours are even with England captain Bryan Robson. But Manchester United win the day 4–1.**

coming back in. Paul Merson had done very well so far. So had David Rocastle. It hadn't gone too well for Alan Smith, but he was still our main striker. The most I could hope for against Liverpool on 12 August was a place on the bench. That was what I got – along with Niall Quinn, Perry Groves, Kevin Campbell and Alan Miller. I did get on, replacing Gus Caesar. So did Niall – at the expense of Alan Smith.

'Frankly, the team looked tired. It wasn't an Arsenal performance. There was no closing down, no hustling, no good passing movements when we had the ball. These players were jaded. It was understandable. Since 21 July, Arsenal had spent seven days in Sweden, been involved in a Wembley tournament, gone to Miami for six days, with an 8-hour flight coming home, plus all the jet lag. These players were drained. They were dog-tired. In the dressing room later, the boss had a real go. But I think he knew the past couple of weeks had taken their toll. We had tried to do too much.'

Graham's last words in the dressing room were: 'We are getting straight out of here. I don't want anyone going off for a drink. And no interviews with the Press.'

According to Marwood: 'That performance and the result had hurt the boss. I don't know whether it was a personal thing between him and Kenny Dalglish or the competitive thing that is now stronger than ever between Arsenal and Liverpool. I do know he was as upset as I have ever seen him. On the bus back from Wembley, everyone was drained . . . shattered.'

When Arsenal's players reported to their training ground at London Colney the following Monday, however, manager Graham's black mood had gone. He was looking forward, saying the team had to get back to doing the things that had won them the championship. Graham is a believer in players showing their quality when they have the ball. When they haven't, they must work hard to get it back.

Confidence on the Friday before opening day was high. Everyone was weighed. No-one was over. But Marwood says: 'It was still a situation for most of the lads where their stomachs were in Sweden, their heads in America and their feet in England. A lot of the players were still having problems getting to sleep at night. Kevin Richardson and Lee Dixon were finding it particularly difficult.'

There had been a week of hype surrounding Michael Knighton's attempted takeover at Manchester United. It meant, George Graham told his players, that in their first League game, Arsenal were on a hiding to nothing.

The luxury executive coach that takes the team to away games left the training ground in Hertfordshire at 2 p.m. Dense traffic on the motorways meant it was 6.20 p.m. before they arrived at their Manchester city centre hotel. When Marwood came down to breakfast the following morning, it was to discover that manager Graham, Paul Merson and Perry Groves had been kept up all night by anonymous telephone calls. Tony Adams was sick with a virus and hadn't slept either.

The bus taking the team to Old Trafford left the hotel at 1.30 p.m. With a police escort they were at the ground in 20 minutes. Marwood left the dressing room to do his warm-up and found takeover man Knighton at the end of the tunnel about to go out and perform his well chronicled juggling act. 'He was like a kid of sixteen about to take his O levels,' recalls Marwood. 'He was shaking with nerves, and the sweat was pouring off him. I wasn't impressed. I have always believed that the pitch is the preserve of the players. The directors belong upstairs. On a bad day for us, United won 4–1. Yet the headlines the following morning all centred around Michael Knighton. To me, that was wrong.'

For Marwood, the journey home on Saturday night told its own story. 'We were probably no more than 20 miles out of Manchester when half the players were sound asleep. Many didn't even bother with the meal we always have on the way back to London after an out-of-town away match. Long before we reached London Colney, where our cars were parked, the video film we had originally wanted to watch had been switched off. You would have thought it was the end of the season – not the beginning.'

# 2
# SMITH'S SECRET

## *Alan Smith*

Alan Smith felt fine when the season started. Even on that long losing journey home from Manchester he felt no cause for personal concern. It was as the early weeks wore on that his fitness, as much as his form, began to worry the man who had finished the previous season as the First Division's leading marksman.

Before the home game against Coventry on 22 August, a match Arsenal won 2–0 for their first points of the campaign, Smith was presented with the Adidas Golden Boot for his scoring feats in the 1988–89 championship year. That award has pride of place among the trophies at his Hertfordshire home. It recognizes his twenty-three goals in the League plus two in the Littlewoods Cup.

◀ **Alan Smith – with the golden boot that made him the supreme striker.**

'I scored in every one of the first eight League games, including a hat trick against Wimbledon on the opening day,' recalls Smith. 'The Press boys converged on me after the Wimbledon match. I told them not to put their money on me to finish the First Division's top scorer. After all, I play with my back to goal so much, anyone who likes to bet on that sort of thing would be doing better putting their cash on someone who feeds off a player like me.'

When last season got under way, Smith was still Arsenal's record signing. He had cost £800,000 from Leicester and in little over a year his value had more than doubled. He remembers not feeling match-fit when Arsenal won the four-club Makita tournament at Wembley. 'I didn't feel particularly worried. Wembley, that time of the year, is always hot and tiring.

'I wasn't physically at my best, either, when we returned to Wembley to play Liverpool in the Charity Shield. But then we went to Old Trafford for the start of the League programme and there were no problems. It's funny when I look back. That was the day most of the other lads were close to collapse. I even felt I had played well. But as two, three then four games went by, I began to believe something was definitely wrong. It was a sensation I had never before experienced. When I tried to run, my legs felt like jelly. From the start of a match they were just not carrying me the way I felt they should. By now the boss was starting to get at me. I wasn't playing well. I knew it. He knew it. I made a point of telling him I wasn't feeling 100 per cent after he pulled me off against Tottenham.' That was on 18 October.

Smith goes on: 'I had scored when we beat Sheffield Wednesday 5–0 and managed a couple against Plymouth in the Littlewoods Cup. But it was way below my ratio of the previous season. Deep down I accepted I couldn't expect to get goals if I wasn't feeling right and I wasn't playing well. After being taken off against Tottenham, I didn't need

15

telling I was now in danger of losing my place. It was so frustrating. My brain was telling me what to do, but my legs were not responding. I wasn't sharp. I definitely wasn't right. The boss didn't say anything to me the night I was substituted in the 2–1 defeat at Tottenham. What was there to be said? I know I went home feeling very depressed. I had been brought off, other than for injury, only on one occasion before that. It was the previous season when we were 5–0 up against Norwich, there were 10 minutes to go, and I had scored twice. But through not playing well? I couldn't remember that ever happening in a League game.

'I had spoken to Gary Lewin, Arsenal's physiotherapist, a couple of weeks earlier, about how I was feeling. He suggested he would talk to the boss about sending me to the Football Association's Human Performance Centre at Lilleshall, where they would assess my fitness.'

Smith, in fact, went into the Tottenham match knowing he would be going to Lilleshall the following day. His appointment was for late morning. He drove to the centre in Shropshire, with his wife Penny keeping him company. The series of tests involved took no more than 90 minutes. Before John Brewer, Head of the Human Performance Department at Lilleshall, had the report that was to be typed up and given to Arsenal, he was able to tell Smith there were no physical problems.

'I was obviously relieved,' says Smith. 'But my other reaction was to feel that the tests hadn't solved anything. I asked Mr Brewer if there was any explanation for the way I had been feeling. He said it could be there was a virus in my system that was taking time to clear up.' The tests included heart, lungs and leg power. The conclusions in the report that went back to Highbury included the following: 'Alan has excellent basic endurance. This area of his fitness is above the average which has

**◀ The sort of touch that makes Smith a scoring star.**

been found in professional footballers.' Smith, when he looks back now, derives a lot of satisfaction from what the fitness experts discovered that day.

When he returned from Lilleshall, Smith went to see manager Graham. 'It was on the Friday, and we were travelling north in the afternoon to play Everton the following day. I had no need to ask why he had pulled me off against Tottenham. I knew why without asking. What I was seeking was some feedback from him on how he felt about the situation. We went through everything. The boss asked whether I was worrying about Penny. She was pregnant at the time. I told him I didn't think concern in that direction was affecting my game. George then said he was leaving me out at Everton. I was disappointed – but also relieved. I wasn't much good to the team the way I had been playing. It wasn't fair on our huge army of supporters either.'

The plan was for Smith to travel with the team to Merseyside – but for him to have a complete rest. That meant not being one of the substitutes – just being a spectator. It was a plan that went wrong when Perry Groves went down overnight with a touch of bronchitis. Arsenal were down to thirteen players on Saturday morning, Smith found himself on the bench, and actually went on 24 minutes from the end of a 3 – 0 defeat.

It was the following Wednesday, 25 October, that Arsenal faced the great enemy, Liverpool, in the third round of the Littlewoods Cup. Niall Quinn was again handed the No. 9 shirt normally worn by Smith, who once more found himself on the bench.

'I don't enjoy being a substitute,' says Smith. 'You can never relax. You can spend the whole 90 minutes being nervous and not even getting into the action. During the time of my troubles I went to Sweden with England and was on the bench for that one. David Rocastle and I were

▶ It's all smiles as Smith gets that champions feeling.

warming up and Bobby Robson was going to put both of us on. Then Neil Webb went down with the achilles injury that was to need an operation. David went on . . . and so did Paul Gascoigne. I came back to the bench and Mr Robson said he would have put me on but for Webb's injury.'

The Liverpool cup game was the turning point in Smith's season.

'It was funny,' he said. 'There was nearly half an hour of the game to go and I was warming up to come on. I felt good. Strong again. I got the goal that won us the tie and instinctively I knew the bad days were behind me. Even now, there is no explanation to the problem. I even had blood tests. The doctor wanted to make sure I wasn't suffering from a rare disease.'

When Italy came to Wembley to face England in mid-November, Smith had been restored to the Arsenal team. 'I had scored against Derby following the goal that beat Liverpool, and there was also one that was disallowed against Norwich. I was looking sharp. Bobby Robson named his squad, and I wasn't in. I was disappointed. After all, England had qualified for the World Cup finals by now and it wasn't a good time to be overlooked. I went to the match. I sat up at the back of the stand after buying a ticket at the last minute.'

Smith admits that, at the time, he had severe reservations about leaving Leicester to join Arsenal. He is Birmingham born, his roots are all in the Midlands and London was really unknown and uncharted territory.

'When George Graham approached Leicester for me, Arsenal had just reached the Littlewoods Cup Final and looked a young team full of promise for an even better future. I felt they were a club about to come good. I was also wanted by Manchester United who were talking money plus players. Leicester wanted straight cash and Arsenal's offer suited them, particularly as they were prepared to let me see out the last few weeks of the season at Filbert Street.

'Three months earlier I had talks with Chelsea. I understand they were prepared to pay £1 million. I just didn't fancy them. It was a feeling I had. At the time, I had talks with chairman Ken Bates, and the then manager John Hollins. But though it would have been a good move financially, I was never really tempted. Obviously, at Arsenal, I'm a lot better off than I was at Leicester. For a start the bonuses are better – and we get a lot more of them!'

Smith would be the first to concede he is not one of the extroverts in Arsenal's squad. 'Have my say at team meetings? Well, team meetings at Arsenal are not exactly a debating society. The boss doesn't usually give anyone else much of a chance. It's mostly just him telling us what he wants. And it's worked up to now.'

When Smith left school, it was with three A levels and ten O levels. He went on to Polytechnic and was a year into a degree in modern languages, studying French, German and Spanish, when Leicester City asked him to become a professional. 'I was nineteen when I signed. I couldn't continue my studies because the degree involved going abroad for a year.'

Food – at least good food – has become something of a hobby with the popular Smith. Among the other players, he is regarded as a bit of a gourmet, and actually admits: 'When I finish playing, it is one of my ambitions to own and run a restaurant.'

When the season started, Paul Merson was Smith's partner up front. 'With Paul, I am very much the target man. I tend to have my back to the play quite a lot. If the ball is played into me, I am expected to hold it up, play it off, and get into the 18-yard box. Paul will tend to feed off me.'

Perry Groves, as well as having a wide role, has also been used as a foil for Smith. 'He is very quick. At Colchester, before he came to Arsenal, Perry was a winger. I rate him now as twice the player he was in his early days at Arsenal. With Niall Quinn and Martin Hayes – both since gone – also competing for places, Perry wasn't able to regard himself as a regular.

⚘ **Look out! There's a Smith about.**

It tended, in the past, to limit his opportunities. But I have to say I enjoy playing alongside Perry.'

Smith says of the towering Quinn, the third of his front line partners by the turn of the year: 'Niall was great when it came to challenging from John Lukic's goal kicks. I know it has been said that Niall and I were a bit too similar when we played together. But not if one was feeding off the other – making runs when the ball was laid back. It is nonsense, as

well as annoying, to suggest Arsenal were another Wimbledon on the occasions Niall and I played as a partnership. He is, after all, 6ft 4in and it was surely common sense to use his height, and play a few more long balls when he was in the side. It didn't make us another Wimbledon.'

The value of Quinn's height was proved in the FA Cup third round on 6 January. Smith was injured and absent. Quinn played up front with Merson, while Groves was wide, and got the all-important only goal with a header. But as Smith said: 'Arsenal winning is more important to the fans than who plays up front.'

# 3
# IN
# RESERVE

*Arsenal's Reserves*

For most of the season, Highbury was foreign territory to Arsenal's reserves. To save wear, tear and damage to the new pitch, the second team were banished to Barnet for home games during the harsher winter months.

There had been moans and groans for several years about the poor state of the Highbury playing surface. So, in the summer of 1989, Arsenal invested around £100,000 in modifying their undersoil heating system, improving the drainage and laying a new top surface.

Barnet, of the GM Vauxhall Conference, have always had close Arsenal connections. Their chairman, Stan Flashman, lists being a lifelong Arsenal fan among his activities.

*◀ Stewart Houston . . . looking to the future – perhaps as first team coach!*

Whenever a player has a testimonial dinner, he is among the first to take a table.

When the reserves played Crystal Palace in a Football Combination match at Underhill, Barnet's neat ground, on a crisp evening at the end of October, the side mirrored the size of the playing staff a club such as Arsenal can employ. There was Paul Davis, still striving for full fitness after injury, summer signing Siggi Jonsson, Alan Miller and Kevin Campbell, who had both been out on loan the previous season, as well as promising youngsters Stephen Morrow and Kwame Ampadu. And there was Martin Hayes. His wife Maria was expecting their first child at any time and Hayes, earlier in the day, couldn't be sure whether he would be playing at Underhill or pacing the floor outside the maternity ward.

In 118 first team appearances before the previous season, Hayes had scored thirty-one goals. It was an impressive ratio, yet somehow Hayes had never claimed a place of any permanency. Before the season started, Hayes, a powerful forward with lots of pace, saw manager Graham to try to establish exactly where he stood in relation to a regular first team place. 'I told the boss I wasn't happy, didn't think I was getting a fair crack of the whip, and wanted the chance to establish myself elsewhere. Before the season actually started, I handed him a written transfer request. I needed to show him how deeply I felt about the situation.'

The first team, when they are at home, meet at a Hertfordshire golf club for a light meal and a talk-in before travelling to Highbury in the executive coach. With the reserves, the instruction is to be at the ground 75 minutes before kick off.

Lee Francis, David Hillier and Al James Hannigan, this particular evening, came in the club mini-bus from Highbury – picking up Andrew Mockler and Gary McKeown at Southgate. The rest, including Hayes, made their own way to Barnet.

Hayes, the target of inquiries from several clubs in the weeks since the start of the season,

▲ **Alan Miller – happy to learn his trade in Arsenal's reserves.**

went into the game saying: 'Nothing has changed. The boss knows I still want to get away. Is it hard motivating yourself in the reserves after you have been in the first team? Frankly, yes. You know you can be outstanding and it won't influence the manager, because he already knows what you can do. But then you never know who is going to be at the Combination matches. Quite often there are managers and scouts from other clubs. So you have to dig that little bit deeper and try that little bit harder.'

Less than a week earlier, Hayes had played in front of 40,814 fans at Highbury when Arsenal knocked Liverpool out of the Littlewoods Cup. He had, in fact, been substituted, saying later: 'I wasn't too upset about that. I thought the system we used on the night wasn't a very good one for wide players like myself and David Rocastle. Also, when you are in and out of the first team it takes time to adjust to the pace.'

The demanding Highbury crowd had appeared to welcome the removal of Hayes to the bench that evening. 'I've had my fun and games with the Arsenal fans,' he said. 'But at the time I didn't give their reaction a great deal of thought. You can take it one of two

▷ **Kevin Campbell – started the season with the reserves and finished it in the first team.**

ways . . . that they were pleased to get me off or happy to see Alan Smith come on.'

A crowd of 390 saw Arsenal's reserves draw 1–1 with Crystal Palace – Campbell giving Arsenal the lead before a Palace side that included Mark Dennis equalized through Chris Powell. Stewart Houston, the former Manchester United full back who coached Arsenal's reserves last season, blamed keeper Alan Miller, a graduate of the Football Association's School of Excellence, for the Palace goal. 'Alan took his eye off the ball,' said Houston. 'He has got to be more commanding. He has got to dominate the 18-yard box a lot better than he is doing at the moment. If he is going to make silly mistakes like that at this level, he is going to make a lot more if he goes in the first team.'

Miller, nineteen at the time, had spent a spell on loan at Plymouth the previous season – playing in the first team and winning approval for some fine displays. 'It's hard, coming back to reserve team football when you have played in front of big crowds,' he said. 'You get used to the atmosphere. Then there is the build-up before a game. It gets the adrenalin flowing. In these sort of matches you have to motivate yourself. It can be a problem.'

Miller drove to Barnet in his BMW . . . bought second hand, he hastens to assure you. Miller trained in the morning, then went home to the flat he shares with his brother for a couple of hours' sleep before going out to play. He talked a lot last season with first team goalkeeper John Lukic, and also benefits from the twice-weekly sessions former Arsenal star Bob Wilson has with the keepers at Highbury.

'Socially, when I was at Plymouth, all the lads used to go out together. In London, it's different. The players are all over the place. My best friend is Lee Francis. I've also had a few nights out with the skipper, Tony Adams. They are a friendly bunch at Arsenal. Most of them, though, are married. At the moment, I'm quite happy in the reserves. But I wouldn't mind going out on loan again somewhere. The advantage for a goalkeeper is that you can be

called back at 24-hours notice. I'm realistic enough to accept, however, that a club like Arsenal, with all their resources, could always go out and buy another keeper. It would put me right back. But you learn to live with that. Even so, if I was to turn the clock back and have the pick of any club in the country, I would still join Arsenal. They look after their young players.'

The previous Saturday, exciting young striker Kevin Campbell had come on for the last 18 minutes of the 1–1 First Division draw with Derby at Highbury. The crowd at that game had been 33,189. 'I can understand just how hard it is for senior players when it comes to turning out in front of just a couple of hundred,' said Campbell. 'It's easier for me. I'm still learning my trade and if I have to suffer along the way, then suffer I will.'

The previous season, Campbell had been loaned to Leyton Orient – playing an important part in the climax to their promotion campaign. 'Of course it was hard coming back to play in the reserves,' said Campbell. 'Last season, I scored twenty-two goals in twenty-one reserve games before going to Orient. There, I managed ten in fifteen Fourth Division matches.

'Initially, I had gone to Orient only for a month. I did well and Orient asked if they could keep me for another two months. Arsenal said it was up to me. I was happy to stay there. The only disappointment was that I missed the final play-off match against Wrexham that clinched promotion. My three months was up. Three months is the maximum you can do as a loan player. 'But I went over for the game. It was great. I felt so much a part of what they had achieved. They made me feel at home. Yes, they're a nice club, Orient. Being in the first team there made me a better player. It's quick in the Fourth Division. Also, defenders try to sort you out. That doesn't happen in the

> Martin Hayes – asked to go and finally went . . . to Celtic for a big fee.

26

reserves. Nobody tries to kick you – not in my experience, anyway. Playing at Orient made me more aware of what goes on around me. But I still need to improve my game by 40 to 50 per cent. I know I need to be more consistent.'

In Arsenal reserves' first twelve games last season, following his return from Orient, Campbell collected ten goals. On 8 November, little more than a week after that draw with Palace, he was loaned to Second Division Leicester. He continued to be a regular scorer. He returned to Arsenal and by the end of the season was in the first team.

David O'Leary is one of several first team stars who rarely misses a home reserve match. O'Leary also likes to watch the youth team when they play in midweek. At Barnet, for the Palace game, he was flanked by John Lukic and David Rocastle. Vice chairman David Dein was also there. So were youth team coach Pat Rice and chief scout Steve Burtenshaw.

All had gone by the time Stewart Houston came out of the dressing room. Houston is liked and respected by all at Highbury – players as well as staff. Houston submits a written report to manager George Graham after every reserve match. 'He is obviously concerned about the squad players,' said Houston. 'He wants to know how they have performed and what their attitude has been like towards playing in the reserves.

'If they don't do it, if they don't work, they will get hurt in other ways – such as coming off certain bonuses. It is up to them. They still pick up their money at the end of the week. They have got to earn it. Generally, I thought the attitude of the more senior players tonight was good. Mind you, it didn't stop me saying to one or two of them that they could have done a bit more.

'For all that, no two players are the same. Senior players find themselves in the reserves, and I accept it is difficult. Some need more

◀ **Kwame Ampadu – when he's strong enough, he'll be good enough.**

winding up than others. Martin Hayes, for instance, you have to keep on at all the time. You have to keep forcing his game. Siggi Jonsson is different. He just enjoys playing. He is a lad who doesn't need any motivating. As a coach, it is part of my job to make sure that a player doesn't let his head drop when he is out of the first team. Paul Davis came into this match looking to improve his fitness. The pace was reasonably quick and I will be reporting favourably to the manager.'

Of the youngsters, Houston was particularly pleased with Kwame Ampadu – a teenager born in Bradford, capped by the Republic of Ireland at youth level, and a genuine prospect for the future. 'He did really well in our youth team last year,' said Houston. 'He came into the reserve side this season and looked like a little boy. So I've taken him out of a central role and put him on the left wing. He has done very well for me there. It keeps him clear of the argy-bargy. He can get up and down without being involved in the thick of the action. But tonight, through circumstances, I put him in the middle again. He enjoyed it. He has got nice natural ability, but he still hasn't got the strength. You look at Campbell, and he looks like a man. You look at Ampadu and he looks like a boy. But Kwame has definitely got a chance.'

Early recognition of that came on 11 November when Ampadu was included in the sixteen-man squad for the 2 – 1 win at Millwall.

Five days earlier, Martin Hayes had become the father of a 7lb 9oz boy. He was given the name Connor. Portsmouth, just before the year ended, were said to have tried to sign Hayes. Their offer was rejected. 'I didn't bother going to see the boss,' said Hayes. 'There wasn't much point. If he wasn't going to let me go, it would have been a waste of time for both of us. I've just got to play on, do my best, and hope that something happens. I did hear he was asking £750,000. That doesn't do me any favours.'

When the season ended Hayes became a Celtic player – for £650,000.

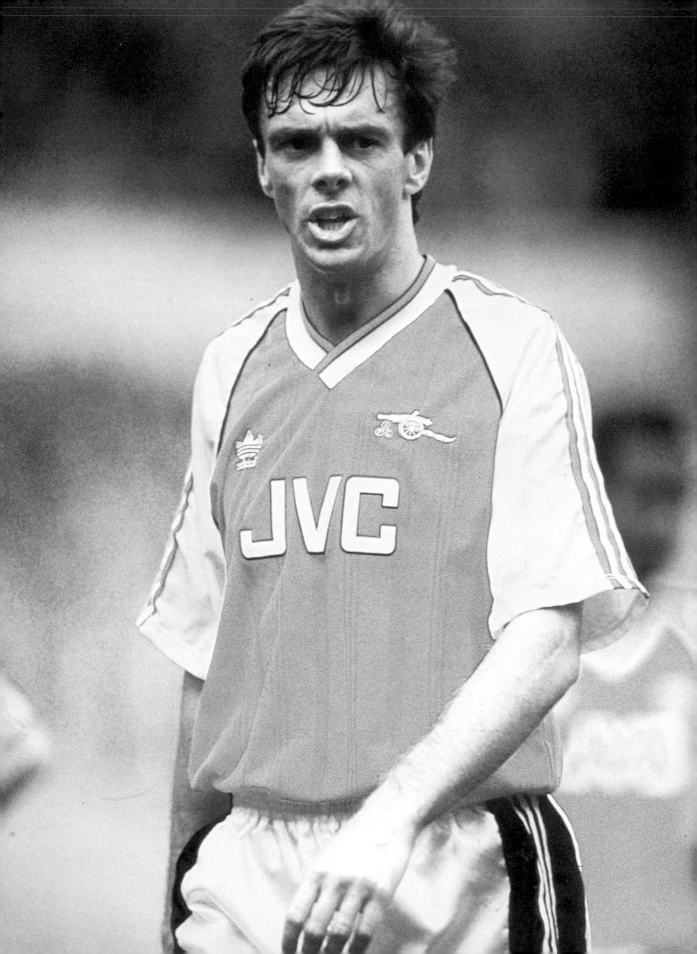

# 4
# RECORD
# SHAKER

*David O'Leary*

November 4 was always going to be a day like no other for David O'Leary. The immensely likeable Republic of Ireland star was not to know it would end in a way that would leave a stain on Arsenal's season.

When the 1989–90 campaign opened at Manchester United, long-serving O'Leary had clocked up 606 first team appearances. When Norwich City came to Highbury on 4 November, it was to be his 622nd game in the red and white he had worn with such distinction for more than fifteen years. O'Leary had long been tipped as the man who would beat George Armstrong's record 621 matches for the club. Finally, the day had arrived.

There are few more popular figures in football than the always polite, easy-to-smile Irish-

◄ **I know we can do it. The determined look that makes O'Leary a winner.**

man. Many observers see it as inevitable that he will move into management when his playing days eventually end. When they started, back in August 1975, with a goalless draw at Burnley, his team-mates had included Jimmy Rimmer, Pat Rice, Sammy Nelson, Brian Kidd, Alan Ball, Alex Cropley and Armstrong. When Norwich came to Arsenal on Saturday, 4 November, they included the present-day folk heroes of Highbury – Tony Adams, Michael Thomas, David Rocastle, Alan Smith.

O'Leary's Friday evening before a Saturday home game usually follows the same pattern. This one was little different to the others. He says: 'About 9 p.m., as I always do, I had a long soak in the bath. I came downstairs, read my young son John a story, and had a cup of tea before settling down to watch *Newsnight* on television. I'm not the world's greatest sleeper, but I've never taken a sleeping tablet in my life. I don't believe they can be good for you. I've heard it said that playing for a big club like Arsenal puts tremendous pressure on you. I've honestly not found that. Perhaps it helps that our supporters took to me from my very first game and have stayed with me since.'

O'Leary, on match days, wakes at 9 a.m. He doesn't need an alarm clock, it is habit. 'I was aware, almost from the moment I opened my eyes, that this was the day I would break the record,' he said. 'There were congratulatory telegrams from family and friends – including one from Tony Adams. But I was also conscious of the need to get 3 points.'

Arsenal always get together at a local golf club by 11.15 on the morning of home games. Heavy traffic following an accident near O'Leary's Cockfosters home made him 5 minutes late. It had assistant manager Theo Foley joking, 'You're a big superstar . . . 622 games. You don't have to be here on time.' O'Leary, at least, thought he was joking.

A pre-match meal is available to all players. Nothing heavy. Just cornflakes, followed by eggs, tea and toast. O'Leary doesn't bother. He breakfasts in bed at home – a plain omelette, with beans, toast and a large cup of tea that has a spoonful of honey in it. He will not eat again until the evening.

It was on the way to join the rest of the squad that O'Leary recalled: 'George Armstrong sent me a lovely letter from Kuwait, where he was. coaching, after we won the First Division title at Liverpool. He said how pleased he was that I had finally got a championship medal and he hoped I would beat his all-time appearances record. I know George meant it. He is one of the most honest men I have ever known. Anyway, records are there to be broken. Deep down, I hope Tony Adams is the one to beat mine. If he does, I would like to be there to make some sort of a presentation.'

By around 11.45 on 4 November, everyone had eaten, and the players drifted off in various directions – some to play snooker, others to watch television. Goalkeeper John Lukic was the ace among the snooker addicts. He usually played Paul Merson ... known as Hurricane Higgins by the others. O'Leary was a spectator at the table they were using.

At 12.30, manager George Graham called a team meeting. He made no reference to it being O'Leary's record-smashing 622nd game. The manager went through the set plays and confirmed who would pick up who at corners.

The players use their own cars to get to Highbury from the golf club. Some travel in pairs. O'Leary left on his own at around 12.50. He arrived at the ground half an hour later.

'I drove through the gate and everyone was clapping. I felt good. I got out of my car and people were coming up, shaking my hand, slapping me on the back and wishing me good luck. There were fans I recognized from the early days back in 1975. They had been good to me over the years. I hoped I had given them something in return.

'Sue Compton, who is now the box office manager, joined the club two years after me as a ticket clerk. I went to see her about the possibility of four good seats for the family. I didn't know that the previous day she had already organized one of the new executive boxes at the Clock End for my wife Joy, my son John, little girl Ciara, my dad who had come over from Ireland, and my brother Pierce who had come down from Scotland.

'I didn't speak to anyone from Norwich before the game, but that is not unusual. I got changed – not having a clue whether there was to be any sort of presentation. But most of the match programme was devoted to my career. The other players were giving me a lot of stick. They refused to believe I was only thirty-one. Dave Rocastle insisted he had seen me on one of those black and white films of footballers with the baggy shorts in the old days.

'It was 2.15, three-quarters of an hour before kick off, when the boss told me the rest of the team were going out on to the pitch a few minutes earlier than usual. I was to wait. There was going to be a presentation. At the time I didn't know, but Sue Compton, on behalf of the club, had telephoned my wife earlier in the week and asked if there was anything I would specially like. Joy had told Sue I collect Waterford Crystal. Sue went to Harrods and bought a really expensive and beautiful piece.

'As I stood in the tunnel waiting to be called on to the pitch, David Stringer, the Norwich manager, came through and congratulated me. He has always struck me as a very pleasant man. When I finally got the word to go out, it seemed that the whole stadium erupted. Both teams were lined up in the middle of the pitch. The boss was there. So were vice-chairman David Dein and managing director Ken Friar. Mr Dein made the presentation. He said it was a pleasure to have someone like me at the club. I was also given a jersey with 622 on the front and back. I was overwhelmed. Also, there was a trophy from our physiotherapist Gary Lewin and his family.

---

▶ **O'Leary tangles with Norwich City's Dean Coney in the match that was costly to both sides.**

'Looking back, I suppose I have been spoiled at Arsenal. All my career there, I have had the very best. That isn't to knock Liverpool, Manchester United or any of the other top clubs. But for me, Arsenal will always be special. I came there for a trial as a kid and fell in love with the place. To stay eighteen years, I must have done.

'So what have I got for all that time? Well, when this season started, three FA Cup final medals, two Littlewoods Cup medals, two Charity Shield trophies, a European Cup Winners' Cup medal, fifty Irish caps, six First Division team awards from the Professional Footballers' Association – and a League championship medal. Off the field – a beautiful home, a terrific family and, I hope, the respect of my fellow professionals.

'The future? I'll come out of the game with security. I don't have any business interests, but I have been well advised, well looked after. I came over from Ireland on £4 a week and the game hasn't just been good to me, it has been fantastic. I know I could have earned a lot more if I had moved on a couple of times. But that wouldn't compensate for all the good years with a great club. And I won't leave Arsenal as a pauper.'

It saddens O'Leary that the general public will remember his record-breaking day for all the wrong reasons. For niggling, nastiness and a mass punch-up at the final whistle. O'Leary insists that Norwich City are about the good things in the game. They don't kick. They always try to play quality football. So what went wrong? According to O'Leary: 'It was down to one player – and one player only. He elbowed me across the face after only 10 minutes. I was standing on the halfway line and the ball was in the Norwich penalty area when it happened. I was furious. I had never had problems with this particular player before. To be truthful, I have never had those

▷ **'Here Ref, look at this.' O'Leary with Norwich's Malcolm Allen on his record-breaking day.**

sorts of problems with any player. What made me even more angry was that it happened on this day of all days.

'The other Norwich players urged me after what happened not to let it ruin my big day. Not to let it be remembered for the wrong reasons. But I was flaming mad. Robert Rosario was closest to what happened. He's a smashing big lad. Strong, determined and a handful for any centre half. He was first to say "Don't ruin your day." But it's hard to turn the other cheek and pretend it didn't happen. Particularly when, 5 minutes later, in front of the referee, in front of everyone, he does it again and the ref says, "Play on." What can you do? What I did was foul him, pick him up, and try to drag him over to referee George Tyson to show what he had done to me. I was wrong. I don't dispute that. Quite rightly I was booked.

'But it still puzzled me when Mr Tyson asked for my name. Fifteen minutes earlier he had wished me good luck and said, "All the best, Dave." Had he forgotten that quickly? The same player elbowed Tony Adams in the face and, in the second half, went over the top to Lee Dixon, and also elbowed Kevin Richardson. I couldn't work out why. It wasn't a rough game. Norwich just don't play that way.

'At half-time, we were two goals down. The boss said that, as a team, we were a joke. He was probably right. We gave away a silly first goal at a corner through bad marking. The second goal also came from a dead ball situation. The boss warned we had better get our game together.

'We pulled a goal back through Niall Quinn. Then we got a penalty through a very questionable handball. Lee Dixon scored from the spot. The decision went against Andy Linighan. If it had been me, I know I would have been furious. But then Norwich made it 3–2 . . . and I was to make it 3–3. Nigel Winterburn curled in a great free kick and I ran in to head through at the near post. What particularly pleased me was that the goal came at the North Bank end, where so many of the genuine fans congregate.

'Right at the end, the ball was knocked down to Michael Thomas. He backed into a defender and went down. He said he was pulled down. The crowd screamed for a penalty, and we got one – our second of the day. It was again very debatable. Lee Dixon's kick was saved, only for Alan Smith to knock in the rebound.

'Somebody shoved Alan as he picked the ball out of the net and suddenly it was mayhem. There weren't any punches thrown, but there was a lot of pushing and shoving. Certainly there was no trouble when we went down the tunnel. Coming off, I shook hands with most of the Norwich players. I said I was very sorry about what had happened. I expressed the opinion that one man had marred the afternoon – and I wasn't referring to the referee. I agreed that, in some ways, they had been robbed. I felt Dave Stringer, the Norwich manager, and his coach David Williams handled themselves exceptionally well in a very difficult situation. In the players' lounge afterwards I spoke to nearly all the Norwich team. The fellow who, in my mind, caused all the trouble, was there. If ever I felt like throwing someone out it was him that afternoon.'

Afterwards, in the dressing room, manager Graham told his players: 'Say nothing. Keep your mouths shut.' There were pictures in the papers and television footage of what happened at the final whistle. In the climate that existed last season, a disrepute charge against both clubs was probably inevitable. It was an episode that ended with Arsenal being fined £20,000 at the Football Association disciplinary hearing that followed and Norwich receiving a £50,000 rap.

Said O'Leary: 'There remained a feeling inside the club that the television film and the intense media coverage made it impossible for the FA not to act.'

For O'Leary and his family the day ended with a Chinese takeaway.

---

◀ **O'Leary shows he's better than a Saint.**

# 5
# THE
# LONER

*John Lukic*

John Lukic started the season knowing Arsenal had tried to buy David Seaman from Queen's Park Rangers. With manager George Graham's interest spread over most of the back pages, it was hardly a secret.

Lukic could have ranted and raved and pointed to the part he had played in the winning of the championship only weeks earlier. His reaction, in fact, was totally dignified. He accepted it was the manager's right, as well as duty, to try to improve his team – and he got on with the job of maintaining the high defensive standards Arsenal had set throughout the previous season.

In the opening ten games, the Chesterfield-born goalkeeper kept seven clean sheets. Even after Arsenal had made their exit from both

the Littlewoods and FA Cups, nobody pointed the finger of blame at Lukic. Arsenal went out of the FA Cup to Queen's Park Rangers in a replay at the end of January. Seaman had shone in both matches, but there was no word of criticism against Lukic either inside or outside the club.

It was around this time that he reflected: 'Of course I still think about the possibility that I could turn up for training one day and find the club have signed Dave Seaman. But it's no good worrying about a situation you can't influence. OK, we won the championship, I'm still on a high, and the next thing I know is Arsenal are talking about buying a new goalkeeper. There is nothing I can do about that. It is literally out of my hands.

'As it happens, Dave is a very good friend of mine. Nobody said anything to me, but I was well aware Arsenal were trying to buy him in the summer and I knew it was more than the usual gossip. Whenever a major transfer is in the wind, there is always someone in the know who will telephone you and say what is going on. There is always someone who will mark your card.

'I wasn't shocked. I wasn't even greatly surprised. If Arsenal wanted to go out and pay more than a million for a goalkeeper, it was obviously because they thought it was the piece they needed for a new championship-winning jigsaw. The way I saw it, all I could do was get on with what I was being paid for. Of course, to a certain extent, it was a dent to my ego. We had just won the title, and there are not many mugs who win championship medals. You certainly don't finish top of the First Division if you've got a dodgy keeper.

'I had made up my mind not to moan or mope. But I did speak to the boss in Sweden before Arsenal's interest in Seaman became public knowledge. Basically, I asked him where I stood. He said he wanted a big squad and he was looking to strengthen. There was no heated row. No raised voices. No argument. It was all quite amicable. I don't even think

▲ **Disputing the claim that he was weak on crosses.**

Dave Seaman's name was mentioned. But the boss knew why I had wanted to see him. We finished the pre-season warm-up games in Sweden, we came back and played in the Makita tournament at Wembley, and still nothing happened, though the paper talk had intensified. It was being suggested that Seaman would be signing by the weekend. I was virtually just waiting for him to arrive.

'My own game wasn't affected. You can't take things like that out with you when you play. If you do, you are unprofessional. Any-way, earlier on at Arsenal I had actually played in the Littlewoods Cup Final while still on a weekly contract. That day, I didn't go out at Wembley thinking of what sort of deal I could get if we won. When the game starts, your mind is focused only on one thing – winning.

'If Dave Seaman had signed I knew he wasn't coming to Highbury to be the second choice goalkeeper. But by then I was under contract for a further two years. That didn't exactly put me in the driving seat. I do know I wouldn't have asked for a transfer.

'The top clubs, particularly Arsenal and Liverpool, will always find the money for new players. You accept they will always want the best there is. If you play for one of the so-called giants, you have to learn to live under that threat. You know you can be in the side one Saturday and the next Saturday they have bought somebody to replace you. It is one of the pressures of playing for Arsenal. You have to come to terms with the situation. If you let it get to you, if you start to accept every little bit of gossip in the papers as fact, your game will inevitably suffer. A positive attitude, particularly for a goalkeeper, is essential.'

It is often said that goalkeepers are a breed apart. It is the most specialized of all positions. The percentage who fall by the wayside in trying to make it to the top is vast. The majority of those who get there are intelligent, articulate and somehow seem more laid back than outfield players. A lot of them are also loners. Lukic is no exception.

He agrees: 'I'm probably something of a loner. I like to think I am my own man. I've got my wife Karen and two smashing children in John and Amy. I'm very happy to come straight home after training. Most of my days are filled with family life. I married Karen in the summer of 1984. She came down from Yorkshire and she didn't know anyone in London other than me. We do everthing together . . . we do things as a family.

'There are occasions when I will go out with the other players. There are times when I will be the instigator of a night out. But it is not a necessary part of my life. I like to get away from football when training and the games are done with. I'll go and watch the reserves. I'll also see other teams. But when I do, I won't hang around afterwards.

'I do drink, but not for the sake of it. Not because there are those who see it as part of a macho image. I'll have one beer, and that will be my lot. I can probably count on the fingers of two hands the number of beers I'll have in a year. I don't drink to excess because I don't see the point of it.

'When the team travel away, I have a room on my own, whereas the rest of the squad usually share. It's no reflection on anyone. It's personal choice. If I'm watching the television, I don't want someone saying they want to see what's on the other side. If I want to go to sleep at nine o'clock, I do. They call me "Anti" but I think you'll find I get on very well with all the other lads. I'm not particularly close to any of the other players, but it's also definitely not a case of them being on one side and me on the other. The nice thing about Arsenal is that we all get on well together. You get the usual ribbing and wind-ups that go on at all clubs. But I've never known it to be vicious.'

When George Graham came to Highbury as successor to Don Howe in 1986, Lukic was one of several players with a contract due for renewal.

Says Lukic: 'George made the point that he was new to the club and he wanted to assess everybody. There would be no exceptions. That was fair enough. I did a whole season week-to-week. You can say I was obstinate. But I was only doing what I believed was right for me and my family. You've got to remember that, while I could have walked out at any time, they could have gone out and bought a new goalkeeper. The boss asked me at some stage whether I wanted a month-to-month. I declined. There are those who will say it was par for the course for me. That I was just being awkward.

'I really don't know what others thought at the time. I know I didn't ever ask for a transfer. The stand I took was no more than exercising my right to freedom of contract. All I was doing was not signing a contract I didn't think was right. Obviously, I felt I was worth more than the club were offering. It didn't bother me what anyone else in the side was on. I knew what I felt I was worth. In the summer of 1987 I signed for two years. I got what I considered was a fair deal, near enough what I felt I was worth. In March, 1989, I signed for a further two years. A lot of people, even inside the club, had forgotten I was ever on weeklies.

'Why did I sign for two more years? Well, basically, we were going for the title and it was the closest I had ever been to winning a championship medal. Also, with the squad of players we had, I felt we could go and win the League and progress still further from there. I had no regrets. There are not too many Arsenals in the game.

'At the start of the 1989–90 season I had no doubts we were capable of winning the title again. My only doubt was whether our frame of mind would be right. But we went into December top of the table, without even playing to our true potential.

'I suppose it can be argued that the Norwich game, the one that caused all the fuss, was another indication that there is good reason for the reputation I have of being something of a loner. There were two ways of looking at it. When the trouble flared I thought to myself, "I've seen it all before. It's handbags at ten paces and nothing will be achieved." A few egos were going to be inflated or deflated depending on who, if anyone, got one on the chin. Not that I couldn't understand Norwich's frustration. It hadn't in any way been their day. The other way of looking at it was that I had never run a hundred yards for a scrap in my life and I didn't intend changing things that afternoon. Anyway, by the time I got down to the other end, it would have all been over – so why bother. I ended up having a chat with the steward behind the goal.

'I can't help thinking that the fans, or certainly the neutral fans, must have been questioning what all the fuss was about. But when you are involved, your adrenalin is pumping. You are out there to win. That has to involve natural aggression. It was just unfortunate the aggression went off at a tangent. But the whole thing was still blown up out of all proportion. What the general public, or the Press, didn't see was both teams afterwards

⏵ **Lukic is down – and eventually he was to be out.**

having a drink in the players' lounge as if nothing had happened.'

It is a common criticism of many goalkeepers that they are suspect on crosses. It is a comment, particularly in his early days, that has attached itself to Lukic in the past.

'I know it has been said that I'm a good shot stopper but weak on crosses,' he admits. 'But what is the definition of suspect on crosses? It is a difficult thing to define. If you are talking of the way I deal with crosses that come in to me, I don't think that is a weakness in my game. If you are talking about crosses that involve a decision on whether I should come or stay, it might look cut and dried to someone sitting up in the stand, but it isn't quite as easy as that. It all depends on the delivery of the ball. If it has got plenty of height on it then you have plenty of time to come. If it's whipped in, you have limited time. It is a decision you have to make in a split second. But the art of good goalkeeping is not the thinking, it is the doing. Once you start thinking about doing something, you usually don't do it. I accept there are those who will criticize me on crosses. That's up to them. Nobody has ever said anything to my face. Probably because I'm too big!'

If there has ever been criticism of Lukic, it won't have come from other keepers. As he says: 'Goalkeepers are like a club within a club. It is a bit of a closed community. When another keeper has a bad time, you know better than anyone what he is going through. I remember talking to Perry Suckling the day after he had let in nine for Crystal Palace at Liverpool. He is a decent lad and I appreciated the mental torture he must have gone through after that match. When you have had a bad game you tend to put everything under the microscope. You usually don't come up with anything. You keep looking at things and the more you look at them the worse they get.

'Any goal that is scored against Arsenal, I take personally. It is the nature of the position. A free kick that gave Norwich their second goal when we beat them 4–3 was down to me. A lot of people thought it was a good free kick. I knew differently. We won, but it didn't make me feel any better. I make mistakes. Every keeper makes mistakes. What you have to do is ration them in the hope they don't cost your side points.'

Lukic was never particularly close to George Graham. But then neither are any of the other players at Arsenal. Nobody gets any special favours and it is almost certainly a contributing factor to Graham's success as a manager.

'I don't think I've been close to any of the managers I've played for,' observes Lukic. 'They know what they want and if you are in the side you go out and do it. Also, I'm not one of those who rants and raves at team meetings. I tend to sit and listen. I might think what's being said is a load of rubbish, but I will keep my opinion to myself.

'I go back to the great Leeds side that was just breaking up when I was first there. They didn't use to have team meetings. But if things were going wrong they would come in at half-time of a game and have a screaming match among themselves. Billy Bremner and Allan Clarke were still there at the time. So was Paul Madeley. He was at the end of his career, but he was still a Rolls-Royce of a player. Paul was his own man and he did his own thing. But he was such a good footballer. I remember once he was being interviewed and the reporter asked if a photographer could come to his home and take a picture of Paul with the family. Madeley refused, saying he kept his family away from his work. I think he was being honest and making the division between public and private life. I looked up to him. I always believed it was a privilege to play alongside Paul Madeley.'

The season wore on – and Lukic continued to look back on the goalless draw with Wimbledon, back in August, as his own best performance of the year.

'I came off afterwards even though we hadn't won, feeling immensely satisfied. Everything

44

⚲ **David Seaman – the shadow in John Lukic's goalmouth.**

just seemed to go right on the day. There are days when you walk off at the final whistle, people come up and pat you on the back, saying "Well done" and you wonder if they were watching the same game as the one you just played in.

'The Wimbledon match was one of those where I know I did all the right things for 95 per cent of the 90 minutes. Everything fell into place. I made the saves, I dealt with the crosses. One stop, midway through the second half, particularly pleased me. A corner came in at the near post and I went for it with John Fashanu. I punched the ball but didn't really catch it right. Even so, it cleared the penalty box and went probably 25 yards. The pitch was wet and the ball skidded up off it. I looked up,

and there was Carlton Fairweather. He hit a volley to the other side of my goal. I had to get across. I got my fingers to the ball and knocked it on to the bar. I enjoyed that moment. I didn't need anyone to tell me that save was a bit special.'

But the man who gave Lukic the most problems this season was John Barnes. 'He just isn't predictable,' said Lukic. 'You can read what a lot of players are going to do. Down the years you get to know their strengths and their weaknesses. But Barnes is so light on his feet. He is incredibly mobile, strong when he is running and he can go in any direction. You feel instinctively that he will beat the defenders who stand in his way.'

When it came to World Cup time, Seaman went to Italy with England. Lukic stayed behind. He didn't expect anything else. A former Under-21 regular and a member of the squad when Ron Greenwood was England manager, Lukic has been on the outside looking in during the Bobby Robson era.

'Different managers have different opinions,' says Lukic. 'It is for other people to say whether or not I should have had a chance.'

By then, the inevitable had happened. When England left for the World Cup, Seaman was an Arsenal player . . . Britain's most expensive goalkeeper at £1.3 million. Within days, Lukic had returned to Leeds – for £1 million.

Arsenal had tried to sign Seaman the day before the transfer deadline. But Lukic had refused to go on loan to Queen's Park Rangers. Earlier, he had turned down the offer of a new four-year contract at Highbury.

# 6
# PAUL'S PROBLEMS

*Paul Merson*

Paul Merson was twenty-one at the time Arsenal won the First Division. The part he played was considerable. He had collected the Professional Footballers' Association award as their Young Player of the Year that season and the title celebrations went on through the summer. Off the field, Merson admits he found it difficult to cope.

Merson, with his untidy fair hair, was being hailed as a wonder kid even before he made his League début as an eighteen year old against Manchester City in November, 1986. Charlie Nicholas said of him at the time: 'Paul is going to be a very exciting player. He's got a good touch and he likes taking people on.'

Understandably for Merson, the night Arsenal won their title showdown with Liver-

pool pushed into the background events of 24 hours earlier, when he was banned from driving for eighteen months on a drink driving charge.

'There was all this euphoria that evening at Anfield,' he recalls. 'But I didn't get carried away with it the way some of the others did. David O'Leary, for instance, was in tears at the final whistle. I looked at him and I couldn't work out why he was crying. But then, as I accept now, I was only twenty-one and he had been at the club all those years, winning every honour the game can give except a championship medal. I realize now just how much it meant to him.

'That season, I had said in November that I wouldn't have my hair cut until we lost. We went on a run and it got longer and longer. We lost and I had it trimmed. I went all through the summer after we won the title without having my hair cut. But before the season started, the boss ordered me to get myself tidied up.'

Merson played in the first six League games of the new season, scoring twice. The previous season, he scored only once in the first twelve games. When Arsenal went to Chelsea on 30 September, Merson was relegated to a substitute's role. He admits he wasn't pleased. 'The boss told me I wasn't playing well. I replied that the team was winning. I didn't argue, though. He's the boss. It's his decision and I knew there wasn't much I could do about it. Anyway, you don't argue with George Graham. And three weeks later I was back in the side. I might not have been happy about being dropped, but I'm not the type to talk about slamming in transfer requests.'

Merson's next spell out of the first team had nothing to do with injury, loss of form, or any change in tactics by manager Graham. On Sunday, 12 November, Jerome Anderson, who masterminds the commercial activities of Arsenal's players, organized a championship celebration dinner for supporters at the Holiday Inn Hotel in London's Swiss Cottage. It was a £70-a-head function, with an Arsenal

◀ **Merson's smile says it all. Arsenal have scored.**

player assigned to each table of twelve. David O'Leary and Niall Quinn, away on duty with the Republic of Ireland, were the only members of the first team squad missing. Even Arsenal's England players, who were reporting that night for the Wednesday friendly with Italy at Wembley, were given permission by Bobby Robson to attend.

Actor Tom Watt, formerly Lofty in *East-Enders*, had dashed back from playing in a charity football match in Glasgow to be there. He is a fanatical Arsenal fan. Peter Storey and John Radford, two stars of the double winning side seventeen years earlier, were among the guests. It was a relaxed evening. Millwall had been beaten 2–1 the day before and there was no reason not to celebrate. Merson, by his own admission, celebrated just a little too noisily. Too much lager took its toll. There is nothing vicious or underhand about Merson. He is, other Arsenal players will tell you, his own worst enemy. Self-control is not his closest ally.

Merson recalled later: 'I came in on the Monday hoping that everything would be forgotten. I didn't really know what to do. Whether for instance, I should tell the boss that there had been some trouble. But he wasn't at training that day . . . so the decision was made for me. I left it. It all seemed to blow up on the Tuesday.' Merson made page one of the *Sun*, who reported: '. . . he drowned out cabaret comedian Norman Collier with drunken singing.' That evening, Merson was due to play for the reserves. He says: 'I got a call from the ground to my home in St Albans. I knew by then that what had happened was in the papers. The club laid on a taxi for me to come to Highbury.

'I felt more sorry for George Graham than I did for myself. I knew I had let him down. He had always backed me, always stood by me. I had rarely seen him looking so dejected. The boss wasn't the only one I had let down. After

They're closing in. But Merson keeps his cool.

all, what happened had followed an incident in a pub after which I said I would make sure I didn't get in trouble again.'

This time, Merson was fined and ordered by Graham to stay away from the club for a week. Steve Bould, involved in the rowdy scenes at the Holiday Inn, was also disciplined.

'I didn't only stay away from the club, I also kept clear of my house,' says Merson. 'I didn't go near my parents' home either. I stayed with my uncle at Wembley. I stayed inside the whole week. Nobody, apart from my family, knew where I was. My dad phoned me during the week and said there was talk that I might be put on the transfer list. I was feeling bad enough over what had happened. That made me feel worse. The week seemed to last a year. All I did was watch television. But I didn't put on weight – something I do easily if I'm not training and don't take care what I eat. Perhaps it was because of the worry. And I was worried, all right.

'I had left Highbury on the Tuesday and the instruction was to phone in on the following Monday. I called the boss, and he told me to

You put your right foot forward . . . Paul Merson with Wimbledon's Laurie Sanchez.

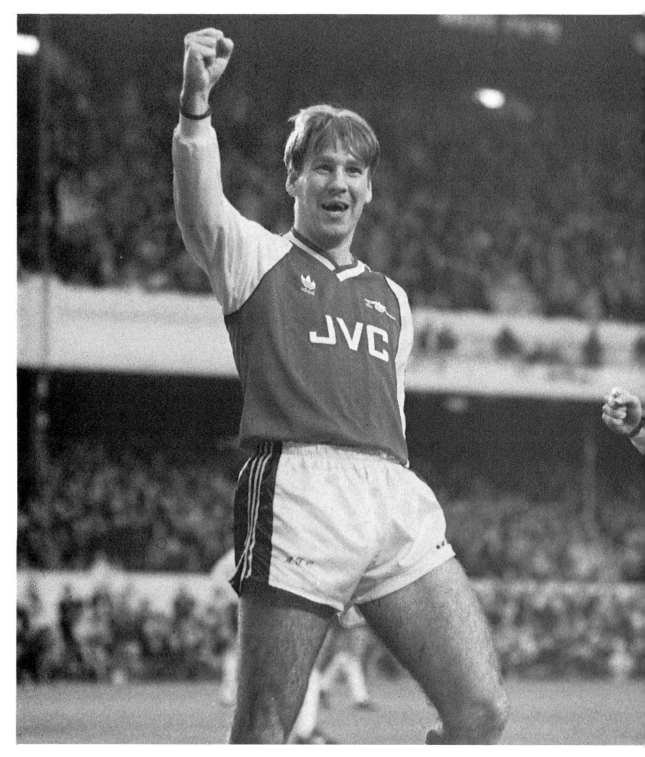

come in the next day. There was a reserve match at Swindon on the Thursday. I played in it and scored. The boss didn't see the game, but Stewart Houston was there. I believe he gave me a good report. I played in the next couple of reserve fixtures and scored another couple of goals. The next thing I knew, I was one of the substitutes against Manchester United, a game that was live on television. That was on 3 December. As things worked out I only missed two League matches because of my suspension – against Queen's Park Rangers and Liverpool. During that time we also went out of the Littlewoods Cup, 3–1 at Oldham.

'My suspension also cost me two weeks' wages. I accepted then, as I do now, that the boss had no other choice. I was lucky it was only two weeks. It is the maximum under Football League rules. Otherwise, I suspect, it might have been more. I expected that fine, and I deserved it. It was just before Christmas and it came at a bad time. I had stepped out of line. I had broken the rules. I had no grounds for complaint. I had let down Arsenal and I had let down myself.

'The other players were great when I came back to the club. They could have made it awkward for me. They didn't and I appreciated it. Nobody, other than George Graham, knew where I was that week. Not even Steve Bould, who I telephoned. I called Steve to see whether the club had disciplined him too.

'It particularly heartened me that, when I returned to the club, the boss called me in and said what had happened wouldn't be held against me. If I did the business I would be back in the team. I couldn't ask for fairer than that. I was wrong, I had been punished, and I knew this was a fresh start. I didn't need telling that I couldn't afford any more mistakes.'

Merson has always insisted that hangers-on – a problem for many young footballers – aren't responsible for the trail of trouble that seemed

◁ **It's celebration time as Merson scores against Luton. Perry Groves moves to congratulate him.**

to follow him in the past. 'I live with my girl friend Lorraine' – they had been talking of getting married when the season finished – 'and I don't go out that often.

'I accept it can be a problem when I go into a pub. I think I have made it easy in the past for anyone who wants to have a go at me. I made the mistake of not walking away. When people wanted to have a go I should have turned my back. I was silly. There is always someone who supports say Tottenham and thinks it's clever to get you at it. I like to think I have learned my lesson.

'After what happened at the Holiday Inn the boss suggested I have a word with Jerome Anderson and ask him to look after my personal affairs. He now takes care of my finances . . . and I concentrate on football.

'I know I have been compared with George Best and Stan Bowles. I find that ludicrous. George Best was the greatest; I would love to be like him. The comparison, I'm afraid, appears to involve my escapades off the pitch. Yet anyone will tell you I train hard – and I'm never late. But I know, and the boss has let me know, that while what happened is a closed chapter, there can be no repetition. At one time, drink was a bit of a problem. I won't pretend I wasn't worried. Every time I have been in trouble it has been related to drink. I like to think it is a problem I have solved.'

Jimmy Greaves and Charlie Nicholas both encouraged Merson to think that he could still be a major star at a time when he was feeling particularly low immediately following the Holiday Inn celebration dinner incident. During that unhappy spell he twice changed his home telephone number. 'The Press were driving me mad when I finally went home. While I was staying with my uncle, I understand they sat for hours outside my house.'

Harlesden-born Merson supported Chelsea while he was still a schoolboy. He could have signed for the Stamford Bridge club, but he

**◄ Merson – concentrating on getting it right.**

sampled the training there, and didn't like it. He says: 'I also had two years at Watford. It was only at the last minute that I changed my mind about joining them as a professional. Bertie Mee was there and Graham Taylor was manager. Bertie is a nice man and I still like Watford. It is the first result I look for.'

As the season wore on, Merson expressed a view that was common in the Arsenal dressing room. 'Everyone has always wanted to beat the Gunners, but now we are the champions, they seem to be trying extra hard. It probably says a lot for the character in our side, though, that we've got results when we haven't been playing that well.'

Another opinion expressed by Merson – also not uncommon among Arsenal players – was this: 'I was impressed by Wimbledon. They all worked for each other and they were very well organized.' It is with an engaging grin that Merson adds: 'They are like me . . . they've got this reputation.'

So what of the future? According to Merson: 'I've never even thought of ever wanting to play for a club other than Arsenal. They are not just big, they are the best. Players come to Highbury, and players go. I don't ever remember anyone leaving Arsenal and speaking badly about the club. Where else could you go? Abroad perhaps. But I haven't read of Barcelona or any of the big Italian sides coming in for me. Not yet, anyway.'

Merson was appreciative of the help Brian Marwood and David Rocastle – himself only months older than Merson – gave him during that sticky month of November. 'I owe them,' he said. 'But I particularly owe the boss. When things go wrong you remember those who stood by you. You just hope you can repay them. I don't need reminding of the best way I can repay Arsenal.'

On the final League day of the season, however, Merson was in trouble again, and was disciplined by the club for an incident before the match at Norwich. Again, there was a question mark against his future at Arsenal.

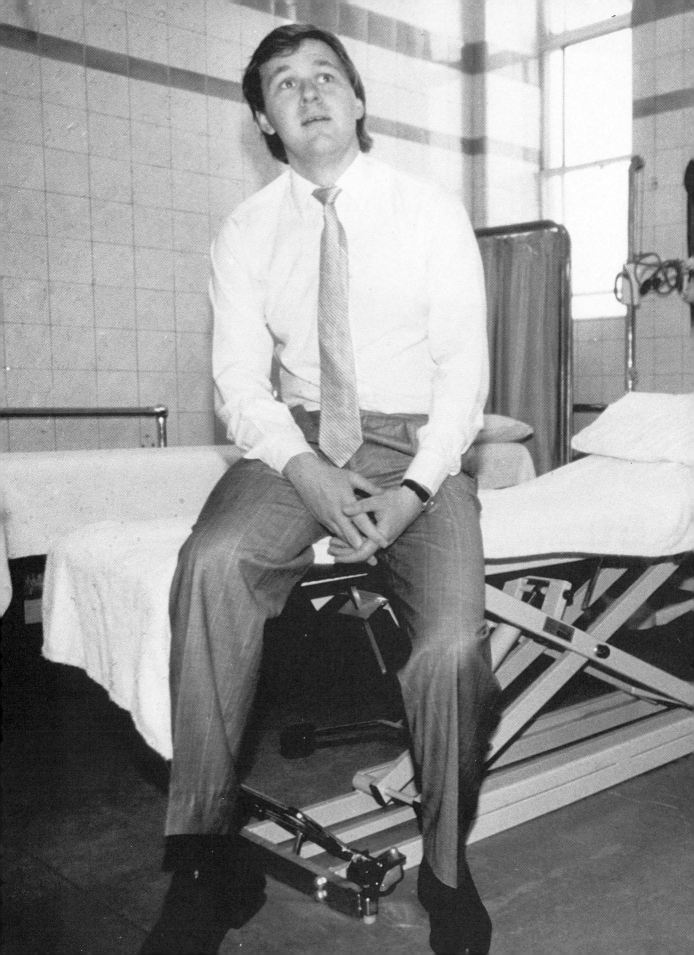

# 7
# IT'S
# ALL GO

*Gary Lewin*

Gary Lewin knew it was going to be a busy week as soon as he reached Nigel Winterburn. It was Saturday, 13 January, and Arsenal were 7 minutes away from a 1–0 defeat at Wimbledon. Lewin, the club's first team physiotherapist almost from the day George Graham arrived at Highbury as manager, saw what happened and describes it like this: 'Nigel broke forward, but the ball had gone possibly just a little too far forward for him. He went for it just as Eric Young slid in directly in front of him. Young's boot, unfortunately and quite accidentally, slid over the top of the ball. He caught Nigel smack across the ankle. The referee must have thought it was a nasty one because he stopped the game almost immediately.

◀ **The players know they are in good hands when Gary Lewin comes on to treat them.**

'I dashed on and asked the usual questions, such as where did it hurt and did he hear a crack. Nigel had what we call a dropped foot. In other words, his foot was actually hanging down. He couldn't pull his toes up at all. That is usually a sign of a fracture. Nigel had also heard a crack. There was the definite possibility of a break. We could take no chances. I immobilized the ankle by bandaging the legs together – using the good leg to splint the bad leg. You use three bandages – one around the foot, one below the knee and one above the knee. You also pad out between the legs.'

The stretcher, something all players dread seeing on the pitch, was brought on and left back Winterburn was taken to the first-aid room at Plough Lane for Arsenal's club doctor, John Crane, to carry out his examination. Dr Crane, like Lewin, was concerned about the numbness Winterburn was experiencing, the lack of feeling in the region of the damaged ankle.

Lewin returned to the touchline, while Dr Crane stayed with Winterburn. It was one of those days. Earlier, David O'Leary had left the action with a hamstring injury. He had been having treatment for it all week. It had been felt the risk of letting him play was worth taking.

Twenty minutes after the final whistle, Lewin returned to the first-aid room. The dropped foot remained a worry, though Arsenal's medical team were now reasonably sure there was no fracture. But as a precaution, Winterburn was taken to the nearby Parkside Hospital for X-rays. Dr Crane and Lewin accompanied him. The X-rays gave the all-clear. For probably the first time that day, everyone was happy. Winterburn was strapped up, given a pair of crutches, and taken by taxi to friends at Wimbledon – he had played for the Dons before joining Arsenal – where he was spending the evening.

By then, the Arsenal team bus had long gone. The same taxi took Lewin to Highbury, where he collected his car for the journey home to Romford. It was almost ten o'clock when

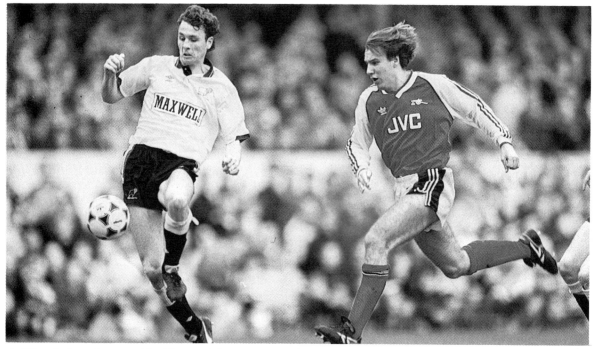

▲ **When he's on form and in this mood, Paul Merson takes some stopping.**

Lewin closed the door behind him. It had been a long day.

At twenty-six, the boyish-looking Lewin is believed to be the youngest chartered physiotherapist in the First Division. He followed the hugely respected Fred Street into the job and the fact that he is liked and trusted by all the players says everything about the success he has made of it.

The treatment room is football's equivalent of the confessional. Players like to know they can say things, and it won't go any further. Lewin's dedication to a highly specialized job is reflected in the fact that when a player needs an operation, Lewin will almost always be there to witness it. It helps him, he says, with the treatment that will be needed afterwards. His experience extends further than the three years he spent studying at Guy's Hospital.

Between 1980 and 1982, Lewin was an apprentice professional goalkeeper at Arsenal.

Terry Neill was manager at the time. He was the one who told Lewin the club was not going to keep him. They already had three goalkeepers, Pat Jennings, George Wood and Rhys Wilmot, and had no need for another one.

'Initially, I was devastated,' says Lewin. 'I had seven months of my contract to go, I loved it at Highbury, and I wanted to stay in football as a player.'

With nine O levels, Lewin had thought about becoming a teacher. It was Fred Street and Alf Fields, who helped out with the kit, who encouraged him to take up physiotherapy.

At eighteen he went back to school to take A levels in maths and biology. At the same time, he played for non-League Barnet and came back to Arsenal on loan when Pat Jennings got injured. In one reserve game, Lewin played against a Tottenham side that included Glenn Hoddle, Ossie Ardiles and Steve Perryman. After Fred Street quit Arsenal for private practice, and Roy Johnson took over the first team duties, Lewin acted as physiotherapist to the reserves while still studying.

In September, 1986, Johnson left and the now fully qualified Lewin was offered the first team job. He went to Street and former Arsenal goalkeeper Bob Wilson for advice. They both said, 'Take it.'

His first match was at Nottingham Forest, and he recalls: 'Charlie Nicholas needed twenty stitches in a knee wound that day. It is still one of the worst cuts I have ever seen.'

Lewin goes to Highbury almost every Sunday. He usually gets in by 10 a.m. A security man opens up for him. Otherwise, the ground is deserted. It is a club rule at Arsenal that if you get injured on the Saturday, don't come in for treatment on the Sunday and then cannot train on the Monday, you get fined 10 per cent of a week's wages. 'In the three years I have been here I don't recall anyone abusing the rule,' said Lewin.

On the Sunday after the Wimbledon defeat, the treatment room was crowded. Winterburn and O'Leary were there. So was Tony Adams, who had a badly bruised hip after a collision with Wimbledon's John Gayle, and Lee Dixon, with a thigh strain.

'The reason we have injured players in on a Sunday is because the first 48 hours is vitally important in getting rid of any inflammation,' said Lewin. 'We use ice and electrotherapy. It is also the time to reassess the damage. Immediately after a game players are so full of adrenalin it is very difficult to judge the extent of a knock. Players don't really feel a great deal of pain in those first hours following the final whistle. It's when they wake up on a Sunday morning that players start to get reaction. They can telephone me. They know I will be at the ground.'

On the Sunday after Wimbledon, Dr Crane came into Highbury. He was still worried about Winterburn. The eventual diagnosis was a badly bruised nerve. Winterburn was even rated as having a slim chance of playing against Spurs the following Saturday. In fact, he returned for the FA Cup fourth round goalless draw with Queen's Park Rangers.

Lewin left the ground just before 1 p.m. He was the last one to go.

The following day, Monday, Lewin got to the training ground at 9 a.m. He likes to have everything in the treatment room ready for the injured players when they arrive half an hour later. It is then that he does a further assessment. He knew almost immediately that Winterburn, O'Leary, Adams and Dixon would not be training that day. When manager George Graham arrived, he informed him accordingly.

O'Leary was sent to have a hot bath . . . and told to stretch the hamstring, as was Dixon with his thigh. Winterburn was put on the mattress to do ankle exercises. Adams had hot and cold soaks. The rest of the first team squad had arrived then. Before they went out to train, Lewin looked at any cuts and bruises and did the strappings. Brian Marwood, Steve Bould and Paul Merson always have their ankles strapped.

One other first team player didn't train that morning – goalkeeper John Lukic. He had a slight groin strain that Lewin had known about the previous day. Craig McKernon, recently signed from Mansfield Town and recovering from a cartilage operation, was also not training.

Starting time for training is 10.15 a.m. When the fit ones go out, Lewin gets the wounded back in. He decides who will have electrotherapy and who will do rehabilitation work.

'At some stage of the morning they will all do some physical stuff,' says Lewin. 'Either go for a run or use the two BMX bikes I keep at Colney. David O'Leary did a hundred miles a week when he had his achilles tendon problem.'

That morning, young McKernon was on the bike. Adams, Lukic and Dixon did some jogging with Lewin. Winterburn and O'Leary were put on individual sit-ups. The injured men finished at 12, had a bath and some lunch, and were told be back at Highbury for 1.30.

At 2 p.m. Dr Leonard Sash arrived. Arsenal have three doctors. Dr Sash is in charge and Dr Crane, who is also the England team doctor, works with him. Between them, they cover the vast majority of Arsenal matches. If they are ever unavailable, Dr Tim Sonnex covers.

'We like Doctors Sash and Crane to both be at the ground for home games,' said Lewin. 'Any one of the three will go away. Not that it is really essential. It is a Football League rule that the home club must have a doctor in attendance.'

Lewin and Dr Sash spent an hour assessing the injuries. When they were not being seen by Dr Sash, the players carried on with their individual treatments. It was 5.15 when Lewin called it a day.

On Tuesday, the players trained at Highbury. They work in the gymnasium and do weights. Manager Graham likes to break up the week. The players who had started the week injured were still not able to train. But Lewin noted a definite improvement in O'Leary. He rated him 80 per cent better and was confident he would be fit for Saturday.

Winterburn still had a trapped nerve in his ankle. He was subjected to pin-prick and other sensation tests, plus individual toe movement exercises. The news, however, was mainly good. Adams, it was reckoned, would definitely be ready to face Tottenham on Saturday. The prospects were also bright for Lukic and Dixon. Winterburn was the one real worry.

For those who did not need treatment, Wednesday was a day off. When there is no midweek match, it is traditionally a day of rest for Arsenal's players. For Lewin it was business as usual, but by now he was pushing Adams, O'Leary, Lukic and Dixon into more physical work. More running and increased ball work to get them ready for the big derby game with Spurs, the old enemy from across North London.

The determination that makes Tony Adams one of Arsenal's brightest stars.

Even so, the O'Leary injury was a tricky one for Lewin. 'I was quite happy the hamstring was OK, but I had to be sure he wouldn't break down on me again after 30 minutes. After the others had finished I took him out on the track at Highbury and ran him hard for an hour. I ran with him – sprints, jogging, twisting and turning – as well as running backwards. Everything he would normally do in a match. I had to be sure. I needed to be certain he wouldn't break down. I decided O'Leary could train fully on Thursday and would be fit for Saturday.'

Adams, Lukic and Dixon also got the all-clear. But the odds had turned even further against Winterburn.

It was 8 a.m. on Thursday when George Graham telephoned Lewin at home to say there was a chance he would be signing a new player. There was no mention of who it was, but Lewin was asked to get everything ready for a full-scale medical. Arsenal's medical for newcomers is as thorough as their treatment and care of injured players. It is the envy of many clubs. Lewin immediately contacted Dr Sash and arranged specialist consultations and X-rays at St Charles, Ladbroke Grove, for that afternoon. As it was, the medical that day wasn't needed. The player had not yet agreed terms.

When Lewin arrived at the training ground that morning he needed to be at his diplomatic best.

'There had been a few stories in the papers about a possible signing and the first person the players ask is me. They know I have to set up the medical. I couldn't tell them anything, and I wouldn't even if I knew. The players understand that, but they still ask anyway.'

Lewin later went back to Highbury, and it was there that manager Graham told him Chelsea defender Colin Pates was the player they were signing – but the transfer was being delayed for 24 hours.

Winterburn, by now, had been virtually ruled out for Saturday. That afternoon, Dr Crane came to the ground to confer with Lewin on who would be fit and who wouldn't. They discussed treatment and the progress that had been made. It is a Thursday ritual. They talked to Adams, O'Leary, Lukic and Dixon and gave them the go-ahead to train the following day. Assuming there was no reaction, they would be available for selection. Dr Crane and Lewin then went to manager Graham's office, in the corridor just behind the general office at Highbury, and gave him their verdict.

They told the manager that O'Leary had trained flat out for two days. They were pleased with him, but there had to be a slight risk of a recurrence. Adams was still bruised, and he would be very sore after the game, but he would get away with it. Lukic and Dixon were 100 per cent. Winterburn was out. After a week that hadn't started that well injurywise, the manager was happy enough.

Arsenal, as one of the game's leading clubs, gets bombarded with requests for players' autographs. On a Thursday afternoon Lewin's car is usually loaded up with no less than four sacks of things that need the players' signatures. He always makes sure he is at London Colney particularly early on Fridays . . . putting everything out ready for signing when the players arrive for training. Arsenal believe it is part of their image that autograph requests are not ignored.

At 11.30, Colin Pates – his £400,000 transfer all agreed – arrived at Colney. He was to follow Lewin in his own car to the medical at St Charles. There were X-rays to ankles, knees, hips, pelvis and spine. 'We took a full medical history from the player, then he was subjected to a complete examination,' said Lewin. 'He was fine. The usual thing with footballers is wear and tear. In this case there was nothing that gave us any cause for concern. At one o'clock I telephoned Highbury and told the boss and Ken Friar, Arsenal's managing director, that Pates had passed his medical and we were bringing him back to the club to sign the forms.'

After delivering Pates to Highbury, Lewin

▲ **A fit O'Leary and new Liverpool star Ronnie Rosenthal battle it out.**

went into the dressing rooms and medical room to make sure everything was ready for the climax to the week – the game against Tottenham. It was after four o'clock when he headed for home.

On Saturday, Lewin arrived at Highbury at 10.30, his usual time for a home game. Winterburn was in for treatment at twelve o'clock. So was Siggi Jonsson, who had hurt his back. As they left the treatment room around 1.15, the players who were in the squad that afternoon started arriving.

Arsenal's stars are no different to the men of Manchester United, the high flyers at Liverpool or those who turn out in the Third and Fourth Divisions. All have their own particular match day ritual. David O'Leary is always the first to get changed. He will come into the dressing room, put vaseline on his ankles and ask for two strappings. He then rubs himself down with oil, does his warm-up and rubs himself down again just before going down the tunnel.

Steve Bould is another who gets changed quickly. Paul Merson has a rub-down, while John Lukic will stretch out in the bath before coming through to the dressing room to get ready. Skipper Tony Adams likes to relax on the dressing-room bed before taking the team sheet down to the referee's room at 2.15. He will then come back and change.

'Every player has his own routine and many of them their little superstitions,' says Lewin. 'I am expected to know what they are and make sure nothing is overlooked. Paul Merson has to have two sticks of chewing gum given to him as he walks out of the dressing-room door. Lee Dixon must be thrown the smelling salts when we are given the signal to go down the tunnel. Brian Marwood will only put his shorts on seconds before we go out. David O'Leary insists on a brand new tube of Deep Heat to rub on his legs. I always tape the ring on David Rocastle's finger at the last possible moment. If players wear rings they have to be taped up.'

Against Spurs, it was all worthwhile. Arsenal won 1–0. And if skipper Adams was troubled by that sore hip, it didn't show. He got the winner.

# 8
# OUT-
# AND OUT

*Paul Davis*

Paul Davis watched from a seat in the Loftus Road stand as Arsenal went out of the FA Cup in a fourth round replay on Wednesday, 31 January. It was a role that had become depressingly familiar to him.

The Queen's Park Rangers programme listed Davis as playing. The previous Saturday, he was in the side held to a goalless draw by Rangers at Highbury. But when George Graham named the team for replay duty there was no room for Davis. He admits he felt hurt ... particularly as it seemed the bad times were finally behind him. Davis had been feeling his way back to full fitness after a thigh operation that saw him miss the early part of the season. When Arsenal won at Stoke in the FA Cup third round, Davis played at left back.

**◀ Paul Davis – a season dogged by injury.**

He says: 'For the first Rangers game I was in the midfield. That's a lot tougher, much more demanding, than left back. I know I had been playing in midfield for the reserves, but there is no comparison between that and first team football. You can play dozens and dozens of reserve matches, but it is a different world. The pace in the first team is so much quicker. You have to be so much sharper in your reactions. I was reasonably happy with my performance in that first game with Rangers, though I felt I was still a long way off my best.

'I knew it would take a bit more time. But I reckoned I had done an adequate job. This was an important point in my comeback and I was optimistic I would be in for the replay. I didn't think I had let the side down. It wasn't until George Graham named the players who were in two hours before the match that I knew I was out. We were at the Royal Lancaster Hotel, not far from the Rangers ground, and it was at the team meeting that I found out.

'He read out the side, and I wasn't in it. The boss didn't say anything to me. But that's his way. He will leave a player out and there will be no immediate explanation. Naturally, I was upset. Disappointed – angry, too, I suppose – and certainly frustrated. He announced the team, then went into what he wanted done, the job he expected everyone to do. I didn't really get a chance to say anything. And anyway, it wasn't the time or the place. I stayed silent.'

Arsenal played well in the replay, particularly in the second half. But former Gunner Kenny Sansom scored a stunning goal, Roy Wegerle got another, and Arsenal's FA Cup interest was over for another year. With Oldham having already ended the club's Littlewoods Cup life, it was disappointing, particularly as the draw for the fifth round would have given them a comparatively comfortable tie at Third Division strugglers Blackpool.

The players were given the following day, Thursday, off. On the Friday, in the wake of the QPR defeat, Graham held a meeting of his first team squad. He said he felt the side had played well, and didn't deserve to lose 2–0. It was a view shared by most impartial observers. He didn't dwell too long on the game – but made the point that Arsenal had a stronger squad now, and players were going to be dropped. When it happened, he didn't want them coming to see him.

'I couldn't help feeling he was directing that remark straight at me,' said Davis. 'I thought to myself that I would still have to see him. I wanted to find out why I had been dropped. I needed to know. We trained that morning at London Colney. I came back to the ground in the afternoon to see the boss. While I had been satisfied enough with my performance the previous Saturday, I knew I hadn't had an outstanding game. So basically, all I wanted to know was why I had been left out. The boss gave his reasons. He said he didn't think I had played to the standard he knew I could. He had expected a bit more sparkle, a lot more buzz. I just wanted him to know I wasn't happy about being dropped. But there was no big row . . . no loss of tempers. On my part, there was nothing to be gained from that sort of attitude anyway.

'When it comes to the crunch, there is only one boss – and at Highbury it is definitely George Graham. Go storming in, and there can only be one loser. It won't be the manager. Stand up for yourself, sure. Make your point. But never get drawn into a situation where the manager becomes angry. I feel there is always a way of getting your point across without antagonizing him.'

With 259 First Division appearances to his name, Davis started the season second only to David O'Leary in length of service. Stockwell born, he was playing for South London Schools when Arsenal spotted him fifteen years ago.

'At that time,' he recalls, 'I was one of a very few in the side who had not been picked up by a professional club. Yet strangely, I was the only

▶ **They're closing in around him, but Paul Davis refuses to be beaten.**

64

one who made it all the way. I came off at the final whistle not knowing anyone was watching. This man came up and asked if I was connected with any League club. When I answered that I wasn't, he said he represented Arsenal and his name was Ernie Collett. I was thrilled. Even though I was a South London boy, Arsenal were my team. I came for evening training. Chris Whyte, Raphael Meade and Brian McDermott, who have all long since left the club, were there at the same time.

'On my seventeenth birthday, I signed as a professional. It was only later I found out I was a borderline case. The club had been worried that I was on the small side and very skinny. Though I'm 5ft 10in now, I was only 5ft 4in then.

'There have been occasions, to be honest, when I have thought about asking for a transfer. Once, in the period when Don Howe was manager, I actually got a transfer request typed out. It was his first season after taking over from Terry Neill. Graham Rix was injured, I was in the team, and the team had been doing well. I played in the first nine games. When the tenth game came round, Graham was fit. He was in and I was out. I was very upset. It hadn't been easy for me to get in the side. But the chance had come and I felt I had taken it well enough not to be dropped. I went in to see Don. I asked him for an explanation as to why he had changed a winning team and left me out. I wasn't exactly enthusiastic about his reply. A few days later I got someone to type a letter saying I wanted to go. I kept it in my car for two weeks. I never did hand it in.

'Asking for a transfer is never easy. When you are at one of the best clubs in the country, it is even harder. I've still got that letter.'

The past couple of years have hardly been a load of laughs for Davis. The best of luck does not seem to have accompanied his vast talent. Early in 1988, a hernia operation hampered his career. But far worse was to come. In September, 1988, television cameras saw Davis

punch Glenn Cockerill and fracture the Southampton player's jaw. It was an incident unseen and unreported by any of the three match officials. Davis was not sent off, not even booked. It was an uncharacteristic moment of anger, brought on, Davis claimed later, by provocation. If the cameras had not been there, Davis might even have got away with it.

He didn't. He was charged with bringing the game into disrepute, fined £3,000 and suspended for nine matches – the heaviest punishment ever handed out by the Football Association. The penalty was more than severe. It was savage. Particularly when you examined the player's exemplary disciplinary record. Davis was devastated. He says now: 'Up to then, I was proud of my record. Referees would struggle to remember when I ever gave them problems. I had never been sent off and in nine seasons I had been booked only fourteen times. At the time of the hearing, the FA said they had taken into account my excellent record. The ban was harsh.'

If Davis believed it would be strictly a climb back to the good times after that, he was wrong. One step forward would be followed by two steps back. His sentence served, Davis went with Arsenal on a January, 1989, break to Bermuda. The trip included two matches. In one of them he picked up a thigh injury. Davis says: 'I didn't see it as anything more serious than a thigh strain. I wasn't worried. We returned to England on the Wednesday, and we had a League game the following Saturday. On the Friday, I did some sprints, and I knew that something was definitely not right. But I played the next day, and that only made it worse.'

Davis played enough games to guarantee he would receive a championship medal, but his thigh injury made the rest of that season a nightmare. At the end of it he was told that total rest through the summer should see him

---

▲ **Paul Davis tangles with Kenny Sansom – once a friend now a foe – in the drawn FA cup game.**

OK for the start of the 1989–90 campaign. For six weeks, Davis did nothing.

'We came back for pre-season training at the end of July,' he said, 'and I was raring to go. Mentally, I felt good. Finally, I thought, all my problems are a thing of the past. I can get back to what matters most – playing football. The first day of training, up at Trent Park, I again felt this pain in my thigh. Initially, I decided not to say anything, taking the view that, as I hadn't done anything for six weeks, it was probably just the actual exertion involved in going back to work. After all I had been through, I didn't want to see it as anything else. I came in the next day, and the same thing happened. I was in pain. I trained for the rest of that week, but I didn't tell the manager, the medical staff or any of the other players that I was having problems. I shrugged it off, I tried to put it to the back of my mind and hoped it would go away. If anyone asked. I said I was OK. But I was kidding myself.

'The next week it started to get bad. The pain was sharp. I knew I couldn't go on like this, so I told Gary Lewin. He suggested going back to see the doctor. My first reaction was that I had seen enough doctors. But Gary took me to see the club surgeon, Nigel Harris. Mr Harris didn't think it was anything to worry about. If I trained and played I should be all right. He thought it was scar tissue and after a few weeks the pain would go. I suppose I was quite happy to hear that – after all I had been through.

'So I trained on, and I played on. The pain was becoming unbearable. By this time we were into the pre-season games and going flat out. I was in agony. I went to Sweden with the rest of the squad and played in some of the matches. It wasn't just the pain that was getting me down. It was also being unable to do things in a game that I would normally manage quite comfortably. If I tried to hit a pass 30 yards, it hurt. I was certain by now that everything was far from all right.

'I spoke to Gary again. I think he knew I was struggling. We came back from Sweden and I went straight to see Mr Harris. Again he looked at it. I did a few stretches – and Mr Harris said there was a cyst on the thigh. They would need to operate, and they would like to do it the following day. Even though I had realized the problem was more than a strain or a tear, what I had been told still hit me like a slap across the face. By now, it was the week before the Charity Shield. Flashing through my mind was that I was going to miss the start of the season. I had missed so much of the title-winning year. It was a stunner. An operation was the last thing I needed. It was a big blow.

'Mr Harris asked me what I wanted to do. I queried whether rest could get me right ... was there any other way. He replied that an operation was it. There were no alternatives. I telephoned George Graham at the ground from the surgery. I told him I had first picked up the injury the previous January. It was now August – seven months on. He could sense, I'm sure, how down I was. He said I must be guided by the medical people. I should have the operation. I went in the following day and had it done. I was in hospital – St Mary's at Paddington – six days. It was three months before I played any sort of football again. I made my first team comeback against Rangers at Ibrox. I scored, but I also knew there was still a lot of work to do before I would be the player I had been a year or so earlier. Even so, I knew the boss was pleased. For the first time in a long time, I felt good. I was contented within myself. I was hoping this was the turning point, that my luck was about to change.'

Davis was helped considerably during a year he called 'the worst of my life' by his girl friend Hope. She has a degree in social sciences and they share the apartment he has bought in fashionable Islington. Paul met her in Jamaica when he went there for two games to mark the country's twenty-fifth year of independence. Davis was among several players with Jamaican parents who were invited. John Barnes, Mitchell Thomas, Brian Stein and Ricky Hill were among the others.

▲ **Paul Davis moves in as Wimbledon's Mickey Bennett gets into his stride.**

He admits his 'bad year' has taught him a lot about himself – and about others. 'It definitely made me more confident in myself. I was lucky that I was able to go home and talk things out with Hope. She understood what I was going through. I think, if you go through a difficult time, it either destroys you or you become a better person. I like to think I have come out stronger and better able to cope after all that has happened. I've learned, too, about other people. It has taught me who my friends are . . . who I can rely on. It's funny how certain people stopped telephoning me. Football, I know, makes people selfish. They have their own problems. It's sad, for all that.'

# 9
# STILL
# HOPING

*Chairman and Directors*

It had not been a good week. A goalless draw at Charlton was followed by a 2–0 defeat at Queen's Park Rangers. Seven games had produced just one goal and that was scored by defender Tony Adams. Still, chairman Peter Hill-Wood refused to accept the championship trophy won ten months earlier would be heading for a new home.

'It does make the odds against us keeping the title much longer than they were before,' he conceded, adding with a touch of defiance: 'It's not over yet though. Remember that right until the very end nobody gave us a cat in hell's chance last year. I wouldn't dream of giving up hope until the last game has been played and the championship has gone elsewhere.'

◀ **Chairman Peter Hill-Wood, carrying on a family tradition.**

That Arsenal were not playing with the fire and zest that was an exciting and important part of their play a year earlier was not disputed inside or outside the club. The chairman admitted: 'We are not playing very well at the moment – and I don't know why. I don't think even George Graham knows. One or two of our players are not bubbling in the way they were last year. It is beyond me to have a view as to why that is. I suppose that having our programme mucked about by the demands of television has not helped. We have not had a rhythm. And losing in the two major cup competitions meant there was nothing to keep everyone buzzing. It is a disappointment.'

The Hill-Wood family have directed Arsenal's affairs from the boardroom for more than sixty years. If Arsenal are all about style and tradition, the Hill-Woods can justifiably claim to have much to do with that hard-won reputation. Peter, a fifty-four-year-old banker, has been a director for nearly thirty years and chairman for the past eight years. He followed his father into the role of chairman, and his grandfather was chairman before that.

'I suppose it was expected I would become a director. When my father died, I had no doubts about taking over as chairman. There were no arguments. Anyway, at the time, I think I was the only one among the directors who wanted to do the job. When things are going well, it is not in any way time-consuming. At Arsenal, the chairman does not have an executive role the way, say, Ron Noades does at Crystal Palace. I don't get involved in the day-to-day running of the club. It has never been any different at Arsenal. We have a managing director in Ken Friar, who runs the business side of the operation, and a manager, George Graham, who looks after the playing side.'

While the pressure built to buy as Arsenal faltered, Graham and the board stayed calm at the start of March. Graham was making it clear he would not bring in new players just for the sake of it. He knew who he wanted and there was no panic.

'If George wanted to spend a million pounds on a player, it would not need a board meeting before he could go ahead,' said Hill-Wood. 'That may sound rather casual, but it is the way we do things. The manager is in charge of buying and selling players. He decides the level of the fee it would be reasonable to pay. He usually discusses it with Ken Friar. One of them, probably George, would telephone me and say what he wanted to do. I would have a brief conversation with him, basically asking all the obvious questions . . . Is he worth that sort of money . . . will he improve the side? If he answers "Yes" – and I would expect him to, otherwise he wouldn't have called me in the first place, then we have the money. I would then ask George to get Ken Friar to telephone the other directors and tell them what we are proposing to do. We have never yet had a case where one of the other directors has said. "This is sheer lunacy. We must all meet to discuss it." That is the way it has always worked, and not just in my time as chairman. We bid a couple of million for Tony Cottee before he went to Everton, and we didn't have a board meeting for that. Mind you, if George wanted to spend three or four million pounds on a player, if he really wanted to break a barrier, it might be different. I suspect if the Italians genuinely offered £4 million for David Rocastle or George wanted to buy Marco van Basten for £5 million we would have to get together. At this moment, it hasn't happened yet.

'For all that, neither Ken Friar or George Graham make any major decision without consulting me. If George wanted to give one of the leading players at Arsenal a substantial increase on his contract, he wouldn't do it without asking me first. If it is a youngster that he wants to reward he would probably go ahead without asking. It is a question of degree. He is sensible enough to know, without any strict guidelines, where to draw the line. Up to now, I have granted every request made by George Graham.'

Some football club boards make it policy to meet weekly. Not Arsenal. There are eight directors, and Hill-Wood says: 'We try to get together monthly, but it usually turns out to be no more than ten times a year. We like to meet when we have something to discuss, rather than have a regular meeting just for the sake of it . . . dragging everyone into town and then having nothing much to say. Normally, everyone attends.'

When Arsenal's directors got together on 15 January – there was no meeting in February – the main point for discussion was the findings of the Lord Justice Taylor Report.

'We talked about the possible rebuilding of the ground, turning Highbury into an all-seater stadium, covering it up, and improving the facilities. We know it will be an expensive operation. The initial estimate was not far short of £10 million . . . ten million to reduce the capacity from 57,000 to 32,000. You say ten million quickly and it doesn't sound too bad. You sit down and you ask "How am I going to write a cheque for £10 million?" – and this is what we are now going to have to do – and it is rather different. Everyone says Arsenal are a rich club. We are. But £10 million? It is a problem, and we will find a solution to it. I'm not looking to the Government for help. I don't believe in going cap in hand. Apart from putting in new seats, if you walk around the back of the ground it isn't that marvellous. The toilet facilities are certainly not good enough. We have also got to improve the turnstiles. They were built fifty years ago. I don't know how we would have coped if ID cards had become law.'

Hill-Wood is an Old Etonian whose polite and affable manner make it hard for you to believe he has sacked two managers. But Terry Neill and Don Howe were both dismissed during his eight years as chairman. 'It was a horrible thing to have to do,' he reflects. 'I had known the pair of them for a very long time

◀ **Managing Director Ken Friar, pointing the way forward for Arsenal.**

and got on extremely well with both of them. On each occasion, it was not exactly something I look back on with any pleasure. But I don't regret the decision that was taken in either case. I felt then, and I feel now, it was the right thing to do. I don't believe anyone enjoys telling someone else they are sacked. You don't exactly like getting rid of someone for whom you have a lot of time . . . someone you have always regarded as a friend. In Terry Neill's case, the fans undoubtedly influenced me a bit. I felt, although there had been a lot of outside influence, it was still me who made the decision. It had to be done . . . because we were in decline, not because the crowd were demonstrating against Terry and calling for his head.'

The Neill sacking was accepted without any media criticism. In Howe's case it was different. Hill-Wood came under considerable fire for the way Howe left the club.

He recalls: 'We had a bit of a problem over the Luton FA Cup tie, where I got let down by David Evans, who was then the Luton chairman. At the end of full-time in the replay at Highbury, the game was still goalless. The two chairmen decided by the toss of a coin which ground we would go to in the event of a second replay. It was done at the end of 90 minutes on the understanding that we wouldn't say anything until after the game. David Evans went straight down and told his manager they had won the toss. It taught me a lesson. Don was very upset. I did feel he was quite right to feel that way – particularly as we lost the second replay at Luton.

'Some days later we had a bit of a discussion and Don asked whether I was going to renew his contract at the end of the season. I said "No, we weren't." That was about a month before he went. He had asked me a direct question. I gave him a very straight answer. I don't regret what happened. What I did regret was when a reporter from the *Sun* telephoned me when I was on holiday in Jamaica. He asked some rather oblique questions about Terry Venables

and I very rashly said I had spoken with Venables. It was absolutely true that I had. He was at Barcelona then. I had asked him in all innocence whether he was thinking of coming back to England. If he was, would he be interested in Arsenal. I admitted I had spoken to him – and it got written up as if I had virtually offered Venables the job. That was far from the truth. If I had just kept my mouth shut that day, I don't think we would have had what followed. It got Don terribly upset. He asked what I was doing behind his back. He came down to my country home for lunch along with John Cartwright, who was then first team coach. I was merely, at that stage, telling him something he already knew – that I would not be renewing his contract. It had another two months to go, and I said I hoped he would see it out. Don didn't like the idea, and he walked out.'

That was on the day Arsenal beat Coventry City at Highbury – hours before Howe joined up with England before they went off to play Russia in Kiev.

'I was upset by that,' said Hill-Wood, 'though I was probably to blame. I read in the papers the other day that he was upset I hadn't apologized or explained anything to him. What could I explain? He knew the situation. I didn't think I had very much to say. I got a lot of personal abuse immediately after Don's departure from Arsenal. But let's face it, one ought to be able to stand up to that sort of thing. I think I have probably learned a lot because of what happened. It made me tougher and more hardened. I don't really mind what people say about me, but you do get a bit fed-up when the criticism is non-stop and you feel you are not being allowed a point of view at all.

'John Cartwright was someone I never really knew. He was brought in by Don and he certainly had a very good reputation. The day he came down for lunch, the day Don said "I've had enough of you lot," John said "Well, that's me, too." I didn't make the decision on John Cartwright. He made it himself. If Don was leaving – he was leaving. That was it. He was very straightforward about it. I respected that.'

When Howe went, chief scout Steve Burtenshaw was put in temporary charge of the team for the rest of that season. Venables and Graham Taylor, then at Watford, were both touted for what is one of football's plum managerial jobs. But it was George Graham who landed the post. Explained Hill-Wood: 'It is true there were others more obvious than George, once Don went, as the next Arsenal manager, but to me, not necessarily in front. Having said that, I suppose, at the time of Don going, I was prepared to give serious consideration to Terry Venables.

'Actually, I considered George when Terry Neill left. I felt then that he had most of the qualities we needed. The one thing he didn't have was experience at the top level. At that time, he would obviously have been a bigger risk. It is difficult to say, but it is quite possible, if Venables had been available when Don went, I would have appointed him. I do know I have absolutely no regrets about the decision we made in the end. We were in a mess when George came. We needed to get a completely new attitude throughout the club. There were a lot of talented players, but they seemed to be split into cliques. It needed a new broom. George Graham provided it. And I think he got to grips with a difficult situation at exactly the right pace. He didn't rush into immediate and wholesale changes. To be frank, I don't think he made a wrong move on the playing side.'

While clubs big and small are becoming increasingly vulnerable to takeover, Hill-Wood insists: 'It would not be possible to buy Arsenal. The directors control 60 per cent of the shares and I don't think any of them are remotely interested in selling out.'

Hill-Wood is not the largest shareholder among the eight directors. He says: 'I have 12 per cent of the 7,000 shares on issue. The largest batch of shares is held by either David Dein, our vice-chairman, or the Carr family, who have a lot of shares in trust. They are a very wealthy family and they are very Arsenal-minded. Richard – he and Clive Carr are both directors – is particularly keen. He never misses a game. He is very loyal, a football fan as much as a director. He doesn't like the social side at all, but is very interested in the running of the club, particularly the playing side.

'I work very closely with David Dein. We get on very well. He spends a lot more time on football business than I do. David is extremely well intentioned. He trusts people, is straightforward and has no malice in him whatsoever. When David joined the Football League management committee, I told him it was a mistake. It is the sort of role I personally wouldn't touch with a 10-foot pole. I have been asked in the past if I would be interested in having my name put forward. I explained that I did not have the time or the inclination. I'm not a committee man. It wouldn't suit me.'

Dein, in fact, had left the management committee before last season. Along with League President Philip Carter he became an ex-member following a major row over the television contract.

Managing Director Ken Friar finds himself involved mainly with the chairman and vice-chairman Dein. 'The other directors make a roughly equal contribution,' said Hill-Wood. 'We keep them informed as to what we are planning. We don't make any major decisions without them knowing and having a chance to discuss any plans or ideas. They are all totally supportive, but will be critical if they think we are doing the wrong thing. We are a harmonious board. While I don't think any of us are mega-rich, it is fair to say we are all well off. If each director was asked to guarantee, say, £100,000 I think we could all do it.'

Hill-Wood discounts the possibility that Arsenal might follow two other London clubs, Tottenham and Millwall, and go public. 'I don't think it is right. I don't believe a football club should be sold to the general public as an

▲ **Arsenal are the champs and Vice-Chairman David Dein can afford to smile.**

investment. I happen to think Millwall is a lousy investment. If you are a Millwall supporter and want some shares, that's fine. But to sell shares to raise £10 million on the stock market is wrong. I just don't think football clubs should be public companies. OK, at Arsenal we have a thousand shareholders. But those people basically have shares because they are supporters. It is not an investment.

We don't pay a dividend. Arsenal will always be a football club. It is what we set out to be and it is what we should remain. Certainly, we are more commercially aware now than we were five years ago. We don't make a lot of noise about it, but we now do very well on our commercial activities. Our club shop has been revamped and we have bought three railway arches, giving us around 2,500 square feet, at Finsbury Park Station not far from the ground. This is now an Arsenal store, professionally run and selling items not all totally connected with the club. Long-term, we are hoping it will be a profitable venture.'

While football – the way it is run and the way it is often played – has come in for increasing criticism, Arsenal's chairman is adamant that players' behaviour has not deteriorated.

'Ten years ago, it is true, the incidents our players were involved in at the end of the games against Norwich and Aston Villa would not have happened. In each instance, I feel what we saw was the result of the pressure that exists these days. There is more money involved, bonuses and rewards for winning are so much bigger, and money always seems to change people's attitudes. It is all so much more competitive. I looked at the Norwich affair over and over again on film and I really wondered what all the fuss was about.

'We were criticized for not fining the players. But after looking at what happened on three different tapes, all three filmed from different angles, I honestly couldn't have gone to any of our players and said "Now you, you fool, it was entirely your fault and we're fining you a thousand quid." Nobody was disciplined by the club. All I said to Tony Adams, when we were at the FA disciplinary hearing with George Graham, was "Look, you tell your buddies I don't enjoy spending my afternoons at places like this. I don't want it to happen again." The incident at Aston Villa upset me much more. It was very silly and totally unacceptable. It was undignified and it was not Arsenal.'

As the final whistle signalled a 2–1 defeat at Villa Park on 31 December, several Arsenal players surrounded the referee and a linesman to protest that Villa's second goal was offside. Said Hill-Wood: 'That was something we had to stamp on . . . and we did. The cynics might say we acted to forestall any FA action. But, I would disagree with that. We could have fined players after the Norwich game. I'm sure it would have taken the heat out of that situation. But I didn't see a case for disciplining our people that day.

'At Villa, it involved the match officials. Referees make mistakes, they always have done and always will, but they are generally honest and decent men. They do not deserve to be abused. I am not being patronizing. Arsenal, after all, do try to set standards. We fined four players, Nigel Winterburn and David O'Leary among them, £1,000 each for what happened that day.'

Tottenham, inevitably, will always be Arsenal's fiercest rivals. Hill-Wood says of relations between the two clubs: 'On my part, I like to beat them more than I like to beat anyone else. I don't fear Spurs. I am not jealous of them in any way at all. I don't think they run their club as well as we run Arsenal. I don't think they are as successful as we are. They appear to make an awful lot of noise about all the wonderful things they are doing. But I don't think we have much to learn from them. We go about out business rather differently. We are a bit more low key. We don't publicize everything we are about to do and say how wonderful it is. And you don't read silly drivel about us every day, about how this player ought to be playing for England and that player ought to be doing something else. It is not Arsenal's style.'

The chairman's sons, Julian and Charlie, are both Arsenal fans. One day, he hopes they will join him on the board. 'I don't find being chairman a strain,' he says. 'I see myself in the role for the foreseeable future – unless the other directors see it differently.'

# 10

# THE

# FANS

## *Loyal Supporters*

A two-storey terraced house, with the front door and window frames painted red, is the headquarters of Arsenal Supporters' Club. There, no more than 800 yards from the marble halls of Highbury, you will find Barry Baker most evenings.

Barry, a computer technician with the builders Wimpey, has been club secretary for the past twelve years. Membership was around 5,000 when he took the job, and it hasn't changed much since. 'It went up a bit when we won the championship,' he says, 'but not enough to make a fuss about.'

There are three branches in Ireland, one with fifty members in America, another, 100 strong, in Australia as well as representation in Malta and Jersey. Barry's position as secre-tary is an honorary one for all the time he spends on club business – and there are not many perks. It costs £10 a year to be a member of the supporters' club. For that, you get a monthly magazine *Gunflash*, use of the club premises, and usually the guarantee of a match ticket if you travel on one of the official coaches to away fixtures. 'Ten years ago, before the football club formed their own travel club, we would have thirty to forty coaches going to away games. Now it is rarely more than two. They have taken most of our business.'

The supporters' club is officially recognized by Arsenal and they get a basic allocation of twelve seats for home matches. These go to committee members. 'We pay for them,' says Barry. 'In fact, this past season I paid £187 to convert the regular seat I used to have in the East Stand into a season ticket. Arsenal's season ticket prices are pretty reasonable. But we are all a bit concerned about what will happen when Highbury becomes an all-seater stadium. The prices are bound to go up and I just hope the cost is not all passed on to the supporters.'

Barry describes the relationship between Arsenal and his organization as 'good'. He says: 'If we need the help of a player or two for any of our official functions I go through Tony Adams. If, for instance, we are doing a raffle there is never any problem getting a player to come into the club to make the draw. We have an annual Player of the Year dance and the players always attend. Last season the whole team turned up. We appreciated that.

'This season, when Alan Smith won our award, we were hit a bit by the Paul Merson affair. I don't think the club was keen on all the lads attending. But Alan was there, with Tony Adams, John Lukic and David Rocastle. Vice-chairman David Dein and managing director Ken Friar also went. The Friday night we won the 1988–89 championship, we celebrated at the club into the early hours of Saturday morning. Theo Foley and Gary Lewin looked in after getting back from Liverpool.'

◄ **Tom Watt (Lofty from *EastEnders*), a keen Arsenal fan, with Supporters Club's Barry Baker.**

Arsenal Supporters' Club own the corner house that is their headquarters. There is a bar, full size snooker table and a television that shows videos of all Arsenal matches. The supporters also run their own team in the Barnet and District Sunday League. Arsenal supply all the kit, including a change strip.

'When you go North and see some of the supporters' club buildings up there, it becomes a bit embarrassing when they come to us. Manchester City, for instance, have a superb headquarters. It is the size of a High Street Woolworths, with waitress service and top-class cabaret on a Saturday night.'

On midweek match nights, Arsenal supporters open their club at 5.30. By 6.00 the building is jam-packed and members are spilling out of the front door. 'We will take £400 at the bar, though most of it goes to the brewery,' said Baker. He added: 'Most of our money is made on replica sales – but not replica kits. The football club won't allow it. That is one of the things that niggles us – particularly as sports shops in the area sell them. Another niggle is tickets. Arsenal encourage us to run branches, but it will happen we have a party come over from Jersey or Ireland and I won't be able to provide them with seats.'

The supporters' club like to think they are community-minded. On a Monday night, they have a senior citizens' bingo night. You don't have to be a member. Any pensioner is welcome.

Barry Baker is appreciative of the recognition manager George Graham personally gives to the supporters' club. 'I see him a lot and he always tries to be helpful.' Baker agrees that the average supporter sees very little of the manager and players. Most fans never get close enough to their heroes to even shake them by the hand. But at every club there is a tiny minority who are known to the players and often the manager and directors too.

◁ **The Supporters Club celebrate after raising £1,600 for charity in a pool marathon.**

At Arsenal, Martin Wengrow is one of the favoured few. He is not a member of the supporters' club, though he has followed his beloved Gunners across continents and through good times and bad. If you called him a hanger-on, he would be furious. He isn't. But not many at Highbury would pass Martin by without saying at least 'Hullo'. After his family, Arsenal are Martin Wengrow's great passion in life. When Arsenal won the First Division in their final League game of the season back in 1971 at Tottenham, Martin was in the dressing room celebrating with them afterwards. Nineteen years later, when they triumphed at Anfield in their last League match of the 1988–89 season to clinch the title, he was again in the dressing room. A manufacturer and retailer of ladies' clothing, Martin says he has been an Arsenal fanatic, not just a supporter, for nearly forty years. He grew up in Stoke Newington, in North East London, where David O'Leary was born. 'Everyone around me was football daft. It was the heartland of support for Arsenal and Tottenham and you supported one or the other.

'I think what swayed me towards Arsenal was that most of the bigger boys in my street were Arsenal fans – and they were the kids I looked up to. I'm forty-four now, but I still remember the first time I went to Highbury as if it was yesterday. The big stands, the atmosphere. I was in awe. It was an instant love affair. I started on the terraces at the Clock End of the ground. I continued to stand behind the goal when I was in my early twenties and could afford a seat. In those days, there was no violence. No crowd segregation like you get now. At an Arsenal – Spurs derby you would just as likely find youself standing next to a Spurs fan. The chances are there would be a bit of ribbing, but never any trouble.'

The plaque on the wall outside Wengrow's home in one of the most select parts of Hert-

Tony Adams greets the fans.

⏶ **The fans' Player of the Year receives his award.**

fordshire says 'Highbury House'. His wife Judy used to go to all the games, doesn't any longer, but accepts the impact football, and Arsenal in particular, has on her husband's life. One son, David, seventeen, has no interest in the sport. Dean, thirteen, is – like his father – a fanatic. He will not have an unkind word said about the club or the players. The pair of them have season tickets in the East Stand. 'I have followed Arsenal everywhere,' says Martin. 'To the grim places, like Moscow and Magdeburg, to the sort of cities where you say you wouldn't mind coming back for a holiday – but never do. I've been with them when I could afford it – and in the 60s and early 70s when I couldn't. I wouldn't like to go too deeply into the things I

did to make some of the trips. It doesn't reflect well on me. For instance, I used to work for an estate agent. One of my jobs was to empty the meters on properties that were rented out. While I never stole any money, it is fair to say I borrowed for a day or two to help me get to away matches. In the early days of married life, I went away with Arsenal once or twice, when really, I should have stayed at home. In its way, it has been like a drug.'

Martin was particularly close to the players in Arsenal's year of the double at the start of the 70s. He has remained close to Peter Storey and John Radford, but keeps in touch with all the stars from that era.

'On the day I was married, Bob McNab signed as a witness. Recently, I had one of those long lunches with Raddy, Peter Storey, Pat Rice and Sammy Nelson. All the talk was about the old days. For a long time before they did the double, Arsenal had very little success. As a kid at school I suffered, living in an area with a high proportion of Spurs fans. At that time they were doing pretty well and we were just muddling along.'

Martin also knows Arsenal vice-chairman David Dein. 'My two boys go to the same school as his sons. David always has time for the supporters he thinks care about the club. I've known George Graham for a long time too. I have three shares in the club. One in my name, and one each for my two children. I would never sell them, even if I badly needed the money. I hear they have been changing hands for as much as £4,000 each.

'In many ways, I reckon I must be one of the luckiest Arsenal supporters around. When I was a ten year old, the late Jimmy Bloomfield coached my youth club team. He was the first real contact I had with a player. Back in 1956 he used to give me complimentary tickets to sit in the paddock. I knew Billy Wright. His son, Vince, went to school with me in Muswell Hill. One Sunday morning, after we had moved to Barnet, I bumped into Billy, who lived near us. He had been Arsenal's manager for about eighteen months, and, unfortunately, things hadn't gone well. But, he told me not to worry. It was going to get better. He was going to sign Don Howe and Frank McLintock. He did, and things did get better. When Arsenal won the First Division in 1971, I was in the dressing room after the final game at Spurs. Five days later, when we completed the double by winning the FA Cup, Bertie Mee, who was then manager, threw me out of the dressing room at Wembley. He had a long memory from when I used to ask awkward questions at shareholders' meetings.

'One of my most poignant memories is of that title-winning night at White Hart Lane. Jon Sammels had lost his place in the team a few games earlier. He was standing in a corner of the dressing room with tears streaming down his face. He was never to play for Arsenal again. He left the club that summer.

'I've known every Arsenal manager since Billy Wright. I would like to think that everyone at Highbury who knows me personally, accepts me as a supporter who cares passionately about the club. I'm not a hanger-on. And I have never ever betrayed a confidence. I'm not alone in caring deeply about Arsenal. There are thousands more like me. I have just been lucky enough over the years to have got to know people directly involved with the club. Dean, my son, has in his room the flag that Tony Adams ran round the pitch with after Arsenal won the championship at Anfield.

'I'm not normally a betting man, but at the start of that season, we had played in the Makita tournament at Wembley. I was really impressed with our performance. The following Monday morning I went into our local betting shop to see what odds they were offering on Arsenal for the title. We were 16 to one, the same price as Spurs who we had just thrashed 4–0 at Wembley. I couldn't resist a straight £50. It was a nice little earner.'

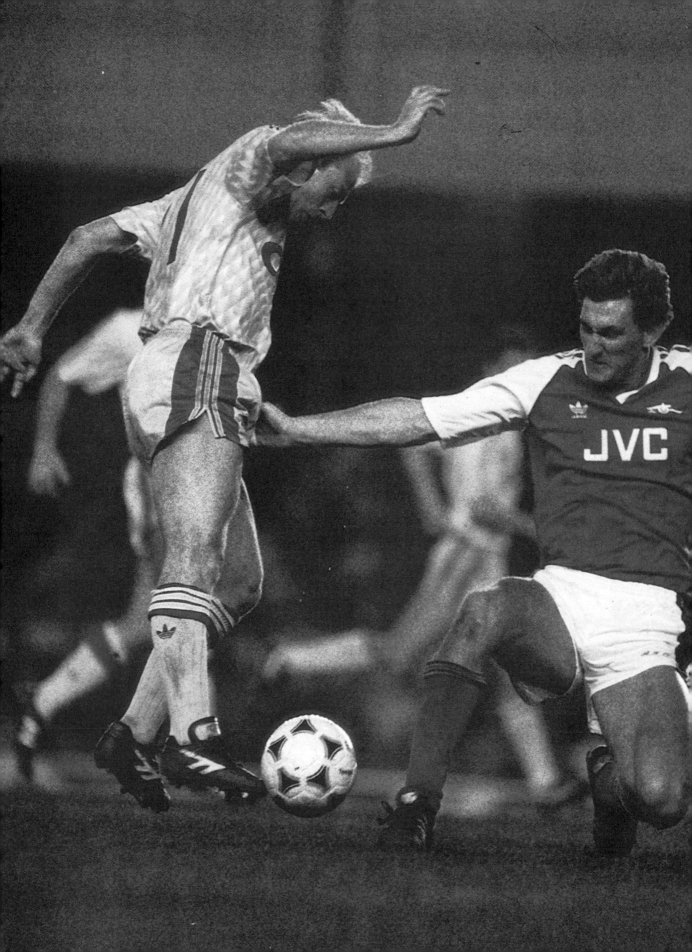

# 11
# HEE-HAW

*Tony Adams*

Arsenal collected £700,000 from Manchester City when Niall Quinn moved north in the week before the 22 March transfer deadline. Skipper Tony Adams lost a golfing partner and a friend. But if it was a good move for the 6ft 4in Dublin-born striker, it was also a good deal for manager George Graham. After twenty-five first team games for City, Arsenal would collect an additional £100,000. Not bad for a player who had come to Highbury as a trainee and cost nothing.

At a club where most of the first team squad are married or have live-in girl friends, it was perhaps inevitable that Adams and Quinn would be good friends. They were born within four days of each other in the year England won the World Cup and have similar interests.

*'Stay away, it's my ball,' Tony Adams seems to be saying to Liverpool's Steve McMahon.*

'Certainly, Tony was one of my best friends at the club,' said Quinn. 'Not having wives to consider, we got out a bit more than the other lads. We had one or two memorable evenings. We also played a lot of golf and snooker. In fact, we were golfing, along with Perry Groves, the day before I signed for Manchester City.

'I loved Arsenal, and it was a wrench to leave, but it had to be done. It became increasingly obvious to me that my future there was a bit limited. I had my disappointments, plenty of them. There were times in the past couple of years when I felt pretty low – even to the point of thinking about packing it in and going home to Ireland. But I had some good times as well. In the first year George Graham was in charge, we led the First Division for a long time and I only missed a couple of matches. I also won Littlewoods Cup winners and runners-up medals. The medal I wanted most I didn't get. In the season Arsenal won the championship, I played only three games. I'll regret that for the rest of my life. The chairman gave me a commemorative plaque, and I appreciated the gesture. But it wasn't the same. The medal is something I will be chasing for the rest of my career.'

It was 11 a.m. on Thursday, 15 March, that Quinn was told Arsenal were ready to accept a bid from Manchester City and he had their permission to go and talk to them. 'I met Howard Kendall, City's manager, at ten past four that afternoon and signed thirty-five minutes later. You could say I didn't give the move much thought. But then I had wanted to move for a long while. A big and famous club had come in, their terms were acceptable, so what was the point in hanging around?'

Two days after that, Arsenal lost at home for the first time in the 1989–90 season – 1–0 to Chelsea. Ever-present Adams reflected: 'It was a disappointing performance and the boss was definitely not pleased. There had been one or two previous matches where we had played well and not got the points. This was one of those afternoons when we got what we deserved. I can't explain it, I don't know of anyone at the club who can, but we have been very inconsistent this season.'

It didn't help Arsenal that, while they were losing to Chelsea, Aston Villa were winning at Derby while 24 hours later Liverpool collected 3 points at Manchester United. 'Villa and Liverpool have still got to come to Highbury and we haven't given up,' said Adams. 'Nobody here is forgetting that Liverpool came from 19 points behind last season and looked champions until we went and won there on the last day. That means anything is possible.'

When players are told to report for training on a Sunday, it is almost always because there is a game the following day or because it is inquest time. Arsenal had no midweek match scheduled. It was in the dressing room after the Chelsea defeat that George Graham said to his team: 'Come in tomorrow, we'll have a chat, and we'll sort a few things out.'

They reported to Highbury at 11 a.m. A warm-up and a few sprints on the track was followed, in the words of Adams, by 'a session of hard talking.' Said the skipper: 'Basically, the boss generalized. He went through what he felt we were not doing and expressed the view that some players could do better. We were away by 12.15.'

Often, on a Sunday morning, Adams goes to watch long-time friends playing for a team called Canon Athletic in the Romford area where he lives. This particular Sunday morning it was unusually warm and sunny for the time of year. 'If the boss had not called us in I think I might just have sat out in the back garden and worked on an early tan while waiting for my Sunday roast,' said Adams. He still lives at home. 'I bought a house at Hornchurch, backing on to the one Martin Hayes has. I went and lived there for two weeks, then went back to my mum and dad. I rent it out now. I missed my mum's cooking

▷ **Niall Quinn tries his luck against Derby.**

▲ **Clash of the giants – Tony Adams and Tottenham's Gary Lineker.**

and washing. I'm not silly. From where we are, it only takes me half an hour, using the M25, to get to the training ground.'

Tony's father runs his own roofing supplies company. It is a family business, with depots in Rainham, Southend and Bow. Tony himself is a director. His role is chiefly to socialize with clients.

In a season when a minority, rather than the majority, of Arsenal first team players could put hand on heart and say their form had been consistently outstanding, Adams was definitely among the minority. He had been a star – looking once more a player of genuine England stature. The critics, if not the cruel 'hee-haw' chants from fans of opposing clubs, had been well and truly silenced. 'I've been having more to do this season,' said Adams. 'Last season we were going forward and scoring goals and I often felt redundant. Yet to be completely honest, I would rather be having stinkers if it meant the team was winning every week.

'Last season, I made a few mistakes. For instance, the Millwall game, when we won 2 – 1, I was responsible for their goal when I slipped over near the corner flag. This season, I have been pleased and satisfied with my form. I have always given it 100 per cent, but if we haven't won, and isn't that what it's all about, I don't feel any initial joy. I suppose it's a bit like John Lukic playing out of his skin and dropping one into the net.'

The 'donkey' chants started early in Arsenal's 1988–89 championship season after he had taken heavy flak during England's disastrous European championship showing. 'Really, the chants don't bother me,' said Adams. 'Neither does criticism as long as it is fair and justified. Like all players, I've been praised when I know deep down I didn't do that well. It is something you learn to live with. Actually, I find the chants quite boring.'

It was when a daily newspaper painted a donkey's ears on to a photograph of him that Adams finally thought it had gone too far. 'It was my mum and dad who suffered. They still look on me as their little boy. People were seeing my dad and saying to him, "They're still calling your Tony a donkey, then." I was personally very upset by the picture that depicted me as a donkey and, at the time, I considered taking legal action. The Professional Footballers' Association backed me. They said that if I wanted to take it any further I would have their support. I gave it some thought before telling the PFA, "Forget it, I just want to get on with playing football."

'I did forget it, although others obviously didn't. But it doesn't bother me. After all, I'm there to be shot at. I'm a big lad. You can hardly miss me. I just concentrate on playing and I like to think I have answered my critics this season. My sister Sandra has two boys at school. The older one, Daniel, won't get involved when the other kids say, "Your uncle, he's a right donkey." But the younger one, Adam, will take on the whole world if he hears a bad word about me.'

▲ **Up and over. Tony Cottee makes a back for Tony Adams.**

Other than an eve-of-season piece with Steve Curry, of the *Daily Express* – 'I felt I owed him' – Adams avoided interviews in the months that followed. He had made up his mind that if he had anything to say, it would be through his football. But he found it hard to contain his pleasure after scoring a spectacular winner as the old enemy, Tottenham, were beaten 1–0 at Highbury on 20 January.

'I enjoyed that goal and the 3 points it brought even if I didn't particularly enjoy the game or my own performance. I didn't play particularly well. Their fans were having a bit of a go and it gave me tremendous satisfaction when I scored. From Kevin Richardson's corner, Steve Bould flicked the ball on and it went to my right foot. I had to come back on myself to volley it.'

Tottenham was one of several London clubs Adams looked at as a much-wanted star of Essex Schoolboys. West Ham was another. 'I came through the various sides at Arsenal with Martin Hayes, Michael Thomas, Paul Merson, David Rocastle, Stewart Robson and Martin Keown. I think they would all agree they joined Arsenal because of Terry Burton. He is no longer with the club, but he was a fantastic coach. When I was fourteen, quite a few clubs wanted me to sign schoolboy forms. I chose Arsenal mainly because I thought I would learn something for two years. My time wouldn't be wasted. I went over to West Ham. There were forty to fifty boys running round and round this hall. It seemed pretty pointless. I came to Arsenal, and Terry Burton was terrific. He was then the youth team coach. It was a great learning process.

'My début in the first team wasn't something I'm liable to forget. Terry Neill was manager. He used to joke, "You'll never be as good a centre half as I was." I usually replied, "Terry, I don't even remember you playing. Were you actually a player?" I was seventeen when he first put me in the side. David O'Leary was injured. It was against Sunderland. We lost 1–0 and I suppose I gave the goal away, Colin West getting the ball more than 30 yards out and knocking it in. Colin Hill was at right back, Kenny Sansom left back, Tommy Caton alongside me at the centre of the defence, and Pat Jennings in goal. I enjoyed every minute of it, and I knew even then that the first team is the only place to be.

'I was made captain when George Graham and Kenny Sansom were not on the best of terms and it was becoming clear that Kenny's future was going to be away from Highbury. The boss wanted to know from me if I was ready. I think he was a bit concerned about my age rather than my ability to do the job. He asked me outright, "Do you want to be captain of Arsenal? Do you feel you might be too young?" There were definitely no doubts in my mind. I wanted the job.

'I don't find skippering the side any sort of a burden. I have always been captain – of my schools team as well as the youth team and then the reserves here. I have always found that having the responsibility of leadership makes me a better player. It isn't a particularly arduous job. Some players, during a game, need lifting. The occasional "Well done" can work wonders. With others, you have to have a bit of a go . . . administer a kick up the backside now and again. Off the pitch, it is mainly sorting out players' match tickets and passes for the guest room afterwards. There is also organizing people for charity work – we do a lot of that at Arsenal – and collecting money for the different whip-rounds we always seem to be having. I suppose I should delegate a bit more instead of chasing all over the place myself. It's amazing the excuses the other players find when you ask them to do something. But I don't mind. I regard being captain of Arsenal as one of the greatest honours the game can give. You are forever being invited to different functions. I would never abuse the position.'

In January, Adams signed a new contract, even though his one at the time still had two years to run. The revised one takes Adams through to 1993. 'I had no hesitation in signing. Where do you go after Arsenal anyway? I'm twenty-three and it has never entered my thinking that one day I might be finished with the game. I suppose I just think I can play for ever. You do, when you're young, don't you?'

As the final weeks of the season arrived, the biggest problem for in-form Adams appeared to be finding a new golf partner with Quinn gone North in his search for games and goals.

◁ **It's a test against the best as Adams clashes with Tottenham's Gary Lineker.**

# 12
# ROCKY
# ROAD

## *David Rocastle*

Arsenal had lost their unbeaten home record 48 hours earlier when the problem that had plagued David Rocastle all season became public knowledge.

On Monday, 19 March, he was admitted to a St John's Wood hospital for surgery to his right knee. It meant one of Arsenal's most charismatic players would miss the England game against Brazil two days later as well as the next three weeks of Arsenal's battle to keep the League title. It hurt the usually bubbly Rocastle that outsiders had criticized his performances in previous months without attempting to seek an explanation. Perhaps the standard he set was so high that any falling-off would inevitably attract attention. In 1988, Rocastle was the Barclays Young Eagle of the Year. In 1989,

*◁ David Rocastle – his season was to end with the disappointment of missing out on the World Cup.*

Arsenal Supporters' Club voted him their Player of the Year. England manager Bobby Robson was among his fans.

It was after his brief hospital stay that Rocastle admitted: 'The knee had been bothering me all season. I tried to play on, although I knew I wasn't 100 per cent fit. We were all hoping it wouldn't be necessary for me to go into hospital, but it reached the stage where I knew there was no alternative. I wasn't doing myself justice. I wasn't right. And if that was the case then the team was suffering. I didn't want a situation where the rest of the side were carrying me.

'It had started months earlier. Pre-season in fact. I felt this sharp pain in my knee the first day back. My mobility was restricted and every time I kicked a ball it was as if someone was stabbing me in the side of my knee. There was no point keeping to myself what was happening and hoping it would go away. I didn't mess about. I immediately told the boss and Gary Lewin I was having a problem. The initial feeling was that it might be a reaction to a cartilage operation five years earlier. Over the months that followed, I tried various lifting exercises to strengthen the knee. It didn't help. Before the Chelsea game the manager came to me and we agreed that, even though Arsenal were still in the championship chase, what we were doing wasn't working. The World Cup was coming up and it was important to be fully fit for England – if called on – as well as for Arsenal. I think Bobby Robson knew something was wrong without realizing I was going to need an operation. When we talked prior to the Chelsea match, the boss said, "You're obviously not happy with it. We won't leave it any longer. We'll get you into hospital now in the hope that we can have you back for the last few games of the season."

'I played in that Chelsea match, or at least in half of it. But the knee definitely wasn't right. I knew it. So did George Graham. He took me off at half-time. I watched the rest of the game from the dug-out – Arsenal lost to a John

⏶ **It's Luton who are under fire as Rocastle gets ready to shoot.**

Bumstead goal in the sixty-third minute – knowing I was already booked to go into hospital. Naturally, I was a bit apprehensive. Nobody knew what the problem was until they looked inside the knee. What they found was that a piece of cartilage had grown back from the previous operation. After that initial reaction before the season even started it had been like having a throbbing headache in my knee. They cleaned it up and the surgeon assured me I would be 100 per cent fit for the World Cup – if selected.

'To be frank, the injury ruined my season. I've come in for a lot of criticism over the year. I tried not to let it get to me, but I was hurt. People who were praising me to the skies a few months earlier were now saying I wasn't playing well enough to be picked for Arsenal,

never mind England. I didn't think that was very fair. Here I was, still only twenty-two, and being written off as an international. The critics didn't know the truth – though for my part I didn't ever attempt to put forward the trouble with my knee as an excuse. My game centres round a lot of twisting and turning. Obviously, with a dodgy knee, I was finding things difficult.'

Inside or outside of Highbury, you would genuinely have difficulty in finding someone with a bad word to say about Rocastle. He is one of football's nice guys. Nobody can remember the last time he threw a tantrum or lost his temper. But as he said: 'It seems to have been my season for being in the wars.' Against Millwall in November, Rocastle swallowed his tongue. Something that was foreign to football is now happening with frightening regularity. 'Frightening it certainly was,' says Rocastle. 'All I can really remember is going for the ball and Lee Dixon catching me accidentally in the windpipe. I went down, and as I was trying to get my breath back I rolled over. It was then that things went a bit haywire. I could feel my tongue slipping down my throat. I passed out for a short while and I was lucky that Gary Lewin arrived in time. Gary said later I almost bit his fingers off as he battled to get my tongue back up. Thanks to him I actually recovered sufficiently to be able to go out and play in the second half. Perhaps that was a bit foolish, but you won't meet any player who wants to come out of a game before the final whistle. The club doctor, anyway, had assured me I was OK and Arsenal are not the sort of club who would have allowed me back into the game if there had been any risk. There were even those who seemed to think my loss of form could be traced back to that Saturday at Millwall. It was nonsense. I even remember one headline that said "Rocky Road To Ruin".

'When George Graham took the decision I should go into hospital, he was very honest with me. He said that unlike previous seasons during his time as manager, we now had cover. That was a fact. In the first match following the disappointment of losing at home to Chelsea, Martin Hayes came into the side and scored twice in a 3−1 win at Derby.'

It was after Arsenal had lost 1−0 at Southampton on Boxing Day, that Rocastle's indifferent form cost him his place. He was dropped for the game at Aston Villa plus the three that followed. On each occasion he was a substitute, and each time he got on. 'It wasn't nice to be dropped and I can't say I exactly enjoyed the experience. It was the first time it had happened to me. I had been playing without a break for three years. Being left out at Villa was a special blow. I had started to regard Villa Park as one of my lucky grounds. I had scored on each of my previous three visits there. Even with my troublesome knee, I was particularly looking forward to that one. But the manager said he didn't think I was playing well enough to stay in the side and I needed a

rest. I think he wanted to see if I would get my appetite back. Perhaps he thought, injury or no injury, I was getting a bit complacent. I was brought back for the Tottenham game, when we won 1−0 and Tony Adams got that great goal. The boss, after telling me I was back in the side, just said, "Go out and show people, me included, what you can really do." It was enough. I knew what was needed.'

There had been rumours all season that Rocastle was wanted in both Italy and France. The talk was that, whether it was Italian lira or French francs, a fortune waited for Rocastle if he chose to continue his career abroad. George Graham just let it all wash over him and carried on working at keeping one of the game's most exciting talents at Highbury. In February, Rocastle signed a new four-year deal. 'We had been discussing a new contract for quite a while,' said Rocastle. 'But the way things were going for me, I asked if it could all be put to one side for a while so that I could concentrate on getting my game going again. The manager accepted the way I was seeing things at that particular period and I was grateful. I got back into the side and we started talking again.

'The fresh terms Arsenal were offering me were very good. The way I looked at it was this . . . I'm still young, I'm still learning the game, and even when the contract finishes I will still be only twenty-six. I was happy to sign and stay. After all, if you accept that you don't know it all, and at my age I certainly don't, then there isn't a better place than Arsenal to complete your football education. I was aware of all the speculation about my future. A lot of people were suggesting I wanted to go abroad and play. None of them actually asked me. If they had, they possibly wouldn't have speculated the way they did. I was rather amused by it. But it probably explained why so many were surprised when I tied myself to Arsenal for a further four years. While I still had a further two years left on my agreement as it was then, the way I looked at it I didn't want to be exploited and finish up somewhere where I might fall flat on my face. I can only repeat that I still regard myself as being at the learning stage as a top-class professional footballer. I was pleased to extend my Arsenal stay on terms that were very acceptable.

'Certainly, I've found it harder in the past year. When I first came into the game as a First Division player, opposing players were giving me acres of room. They didn't know me. I didn't have a reputation. I was just another youngster who had arrived on the scene trying to make a name for himself. The experienced professionals must have seen dozens like me. As the years go by and you start to make a bit of a name for yourself, it's obvious you are going to be marked tighter and tighter. You are no longer an unknown. The opposition are waiting for you. This season, there have been times when people have been queuing up to take the ball off me. That was a part of my development the critics didn't pick up. You can't beat three men all the time.

'Hopefully, it has been noticed the number of times I have taken defenders out of position before providing the pass to put other players in. This season, for instance, I think Lee Dixon has got forward into threatening positions more times than I have. I just feel I ought to get a bit of credit for that. Defenders have been concentrating on me, and it has given Lee his chance. They forget how good a player Lee is coming forward. If I come inside, it leaves the space for him. There seem to be those who expect you to beat three and four defenders all the time. If only the game was like that. As you progress, you realize it can be just as effective to do the simple thing.

'I have never forgotten something Graham Rix told me when I first came into the side in the 1984–85 season. He said, "It's not the first year, it's not the second year . . . it's the third, fourth and fifth years you make your mark as a player." I've discovered how true that statement is. For those initial two years you are allowed to get on with the game. Defenders

don't pick you up. Then, suddenly, you are a marked man. The time and space that were there when you first came into the side are gone. You learn, or you go under. Tony Daley, of Aston Villa, and Matthew Le Tissier, of Southampton, have captured a lot of attention this season. Good luck to them. They are exciting young players. They got their chance and they took it. But over the next two or three seasons they will find it gets much tighter and tougher. Then, we will see how good they really are.

'For me, Arsenal winning the championship was bound to make it even harder. But you expect that. Anyway, we are not a club the directors, manager or fans expect to see in mid-table. We are the Arsenal. We have to be up there challenging Liverpool or whoever else is the team of the moment. Not one year – but every year. Arsenal players know that being also-rans is unacceptable. Yet if everyone at Highbury is honest with themselves, we have not played very well this season. It only highlights the terrific professionalism that runs through the club that we have remained in contention for so long. There are other big clubs, Manchester United are one, who would be delighted to have had the sort of League season we have.

'When we won the title, I didn't really appreciate at first what it meant. I suppose it wasn't that it came easy for me – more that it came early. It sank in, when we went on the parade with the championship trophy around North London. I saw grown men crying. They had waited so long for it to happen. Then there was David O'Leary, a great player who had been chasing a League championship medal all his career . . . finally getting one at the age of thirty-plus. I look at Bryan Robson, a world-class player, and he hasn't got a championship medal. I look at myself. Here I am, twenty-two years old, I have played for my country,

▷ **Rocastle's around – and that means trouble for someone.**

98

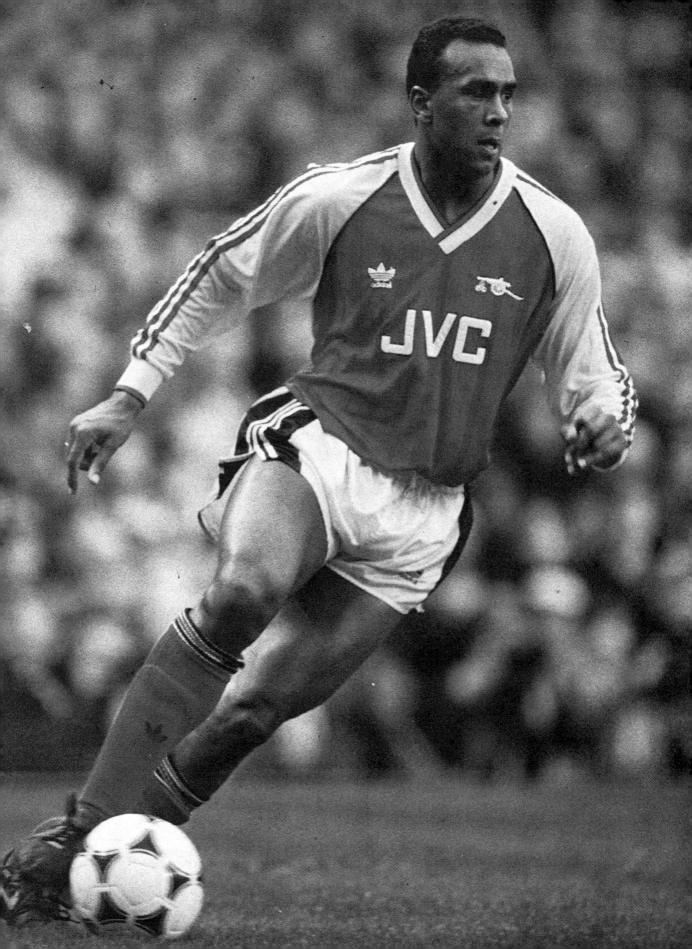

▲ **This is one hurdle Rocastle should have no trouble clearing.**

I've got a Littlewoods Cup medal and a First Division championship medal. You give it a bit of thought and you realize how lucky you are. I'm not satisfied with what I have done so far. I want to go on being a winner. Aren't the great players the ones who want to go on doing it over and over again?

'Money didn't motivate me when it came to Arsenal winning the title. But it was nice to be able to buy some things for my mother. My father died when I was five and it was a struggle for her to bring up the family. I became a father figure to my younger brothers and sisters very early in life. Football has given me a good living and the means to look after them. Football has meant that life doesn't have to be a struggle. I like being a professional footballer and I won't abuse something I regard as a privilege.'

Rocastle recently bought a house in the select London suburb of Mill Hill where he now lives with his girl friend Janet and baby daughter Melissa. It is a lifetime away from the tough area of Millwall where he grew up. He was actually at Millwall as a schoolboy and reminds you – as well as himself – that Bob Pearson, who followed John Docherty as manager, was the man who told him he wouldn't make it as a player. 'I got one of those letters from the club that says, "Thanks, but no thanks. We hope you make it somewhere else." I was thirteen at the time, and to be honest I wasn't as intense about the game as I might have been. After that, I concentrated on my school work and let the football take care of itself. I was fourteen when Arsenal spotted me playing for my District side and took me to Highbury. Terry Neill signed me as an apprentice and I became a full professional at eighteen.'

Being a minority black player has never given Rocastle any problems. He reflects: 'When I came to Arsenal, Paul Davis and Viv Anderson were already established. Possibly that helped smooth the way for me. Anyway, if you look around there are not many clubs now without at least one black player. It must have been hard, though, in the early days for lads like Cyrille Regis and the late Laurie Cunningham. They were trail blazers. Certainly, I don't get any racist abuse from the terraces when we play away these days. Mind you, it would be hard to hurl abuse at players on the other side when you've got black players on your own side. There has been some in the past . . . aimed, more than anything, at trying to put you off your game.

'Like all players, I prefer some grounds more than others. I love playing at Manchester United, Liverpool, Aston Villa and Tottenham. There are others you go to and say to yourself, "Hell, I wish we weren't playing here today." I have never liked going to West Ham. It is so cramped. There never seems to be any space. And I'm not a lover of Chelsea. You go there and the fans are so far away. There is never any real atmosphere.'

Rocastle readily admits last season was an indifferent one for him. 'But if someone had said to me at the start of my career I was going to have four memorable years and one bad one, I think I might have settled for that. I know I haven't become a bad player overnight. George Graham made the point that even though I've not had a good season, if I became available for transfer, there would be a rush to buy me. I appreciated that – the same as I appreciated the confidence he showed in me with the new contract. He knows I am Arsenal through and through.

'How much am I worth? I haven't a clue. I've seen the figure £4 million mentioned, but I don't take any notice of that. I know I have been knocked by the very same people who were saying a year earlier that I should play for England. I know the people who matter most are Arsenal Football Club. They pay my wages.

'During the bad spell, I had a lot of encouraging fan mail. Also, I'm afraid, some poison pen letters. They claimed to be Arsenal fans, and they said my form was a disgrace. I found that hard to take. But then these were the same people who were writing to the club last year and saying we would never win the title. This time they were saying the team was the worst for a long time and I should leave the club. Then you see signed at the bottom – "A loyal Arsenal supporter". It made me wonder if they were not from that lot, Tottenham, down the road.'

Rocastle is highly regarded by everyone at Arsenal. His warm personality makes him a friend to all. But he readily admits his closest pal is Michael Thomas. 'We came through the South London District side at the same time and we were at Millwall together. I'm godfather to his baby Dorrian, and he is godfather to my little girl. I'm very close to all the players at Arsenal. We have a family atmosphere. You could say we are all brothers. It is one reason why I was happy to stay for a further four years.'

# 13
# PERRY
# WHO?

*Perry Groves*

Perry Groves became an Arsenal player in September 1986. He was manager George Graham's first signing. The fee paid to Fourth Division Colchester was a modest £65,000. Inevitably, the question asked was – Perry who?

Groves, Bow-born, was twenty-one at the time. With his crew-cut hair and fresh-faced look he could have been mistaken for a boy marine. But his pace was electric and his potential enormous. He was a shrewd buy. He could play on either wing and in 156 League games for the Essex club had scored twenty-six goals. Perry's background was pure football. His father had been a good non-League player and he was distantly related to the former Leyton Orient and Arsenal star Vic Groves.

◀ **Chelsea's Gareth Hall lunges in – but Groves is away.**

When the 1989–90 season arrived, Groves had collected a First Division championship medal, a Littlewoods Cup winners medal and a Littlewoods Cup runners-up medal. On 24 March, Arsenal won 3–0 at Derby and manager Graham described Groves as ... 'Outstanding. Arsenal's best player.' No longer were fans or opposing defenders asking – Perry who?

Groves doesn't have a star complex. He is totally uncomplicated and has never forgotten his humble beginnings in the Fourth Division. He still lives in Colchester, with his wife Mandy and baby son Lewis. Now, though, it is in a detached four-bedroom house in one of the best parts of town. 'I bought my first home when I moved to Arsenal,' he says. 'To be perfectly honest I couldn't afford a house when I was playing for Colchester. I wasn't even on the phone.

'When I first joined Colchester, a few of the older players were on good money. As much as £300 a week. That isn't bad when you consider it was nearly ten years ago. But the club were losing £4,000 a week and they had to cut their wage bill. They got rid of all the older players, the ones they reckoned were the big earners. Cyril Lea, who was then the manager, had developed a good youth policy. He brought through a lot of young players – including me. My first professional contract, when I was seventeen, was for £55 a week. It later went to £75 and the most I ever earned at Colchester was £150 a week. A lot of my mates, people I was at school with, were coming home at the end of the week with a lot more in the wage packet than I was. One was a carpenter, another the manager of a supermarket. They used to think I was a big earner. At that time I didn't tell them otherwise.

'When I initially got in the first team, the bonus structure allowed for £60 a week if we were in the top six. They scrapped the bonuses and for a while we didn't get anything at all. They were eventually brought back – £10 a week for being in the top six. In my time there

we were always a top eight bet. But it didn't do to rely on the bonuses.'

Groves hasn't only experienced hard times. He also knows what it feels like to be rejected by a club. As a schoolboy of sixteen he was turned away at Wolves. 'John Barnwell was manager. He told me they had no money and could only take on local lads. I suppose it might have been a way of saying "Sorry son . . . but". After that, I went for loads of trials. I tried my luck at Peterborough, Ipswich, Luton, Norwich and Colchester. I decided that whoever offered the first contract would get me. It happened to be Colchester. Bobby Roberts signed me.

'I was twenty when I heard there were a few clubs interested in me. Cyril Lea, who had followed Allan Hunter as manager, felt we had a good chance of promotion. He didn't want to lose his good youngsters – players he had developed over a couple of years. Six of us were twenty or under and he felt he had a side with a future. Then, sadly, he got the sack. The club agreed to put me on the transfer list and a few months later I signed for Arsenal.

'At Colchester, we usually played our home games on a Friday night. It meant there were always a lot of managers and scouts watching. Crystal Palace, I knew, were very interested. Ipswich, Norwich, Sunderland and Middlesbrough were also frequent visitors. I had always felt that I might go somewhere like Palace or Norwich. Then, if I made it, a big club such as Arsenal would come in for me.

'To go from Colchester to Arsenal was a giant step. I travelled to Highbury from Colchester on a Thursday morning and was an Arsenal player by lunch-time. George Graham didn't have to sell the club to me. Really, it was ironic. I had been due to play in the Littlewoods Cup for Colchester at Peterborough 48 hours earlier. But my grandmother died and I had to telephone the club and say I couldn't play. The following day, the Wednesday, I got a

◀ **Groves gets in with a right as Villa's Kevin Gage looks on.**

105

message from Mike Walker, who was care-taker manager, telling me a fee had been agreed with Arsenal and I was to go for talks there the next day. I thought it was a wind-up.

'That season finished with me playing at Wembley in the Littlewoods Cup Final win over Liverpool. If I had played that Tuesday night at Peterborough I wouldn't have been eligible.

'Has this been my best season? It has certainly been my most consistent. I was pleased about the goal I scored at Derby as well as with my overall performance. We were three up at half-time and two of the goals came from my crosses. It doesn't do any harm, either, if the boss thinks you did well.'

Groves, with David Rocastle injured, played on the right wing at Derby. It is not his favourite position. He prefers playing down the middle. 'You get involved in the game a lot more. On the wing you tend to drift in and out. If I have to play wide, I prefer the right side. I suppose the thing I give the team when I am playing is pace. It is easier away from home. You get more space. It was something I appreciated in the game at Derby. If we are defending a lot, the guys at the back know that if there is someone like me or Martin Hayes up front they can knock the ball forward and there is a fair chance we will get on the end of it.'

In his early days at Arsenal, Groves described himself as a 'nobody'. He still feels it was a reasonably accurate description. 'At that time, Charlie Nicholas, Graham Rix, Tony Adams, Paul Davis and David Rocastle were established big names. The boss had been at the club a couple of months and everyone expected his first signing to be a famous name. It turned out to be me. Very flattering. But while I came in knowing who they were, I must have been like the man in the moon to them. Yet from the day I arrived here, I've never been made to feel inferior. I've always been made to

▷ **Perry Groves and Danny Maddix of QPR. Groves has made up his mind he will win this one.**

106

feel at home. In three years I have never felt insecure. Of course there is pressure, but it is on the big stars as well as on me. Pressure? I could still be at Colchester where it has been a losing battle to stay in the League. Players there have been fighting for their living.'

Travelling away with Arsenal and playing in an away match for Colchester is a bit like comparing a holiday in Margate with one in Marbella. After training on Friday morning at London Colney before the Derby game, the Arsenal squad travelled to the East Midlands that afternoon on an executive coach – the one they always use – watching video films and with waiter service. When they are both playing, Groves rooms with Paul Merson. Merson was injured, didn't travel, and Groves shared with Lee Dixon at the luxury hotel Arsenal favour on the outskirts of Derby. After dinner – soup, chicken and fruit salad – Groves was in his room just after 9 p.m. But he did not go to sleep immediately. Home or away on a Friday night he likes to relax watching television. The programmes this past season were usually the same . . . *Cheers, Roseanne* and *Whose Line Is It Anyway?*

The journey home from an away game is always better when you win. It is the same whether you are Arsenal or Colchester, Liverpool or Lincoln. It is just that if you are Arsenal or Liverpool there is a little more luxury. On the way back from Derby it was waiter service as usual. Smoked salmon or prawn cocktail was followed by a choice of beef, chicken or steak and kidney pie. To finish, gateaux or apple pie with custard. Alcohol is forbidden by law.

It was different at Colchester. Groves remembers: 'If we had been playing at Hartlepool on a Tuesday night, we would have left Layer Road at 8.15 a.m. The journey took about 6 hours. On the way we would stop at a motorway café for something to eat. The club would give you two or three quid for food. We would usually go to a hotel for tea and toast before going on to play the game. Then, straight back afterwards, with a stop at a fish and chip shop on the way.

We'd be back in Colchester about five o'clock the next morning. You got used to it. And it's certainly not a criticism of Colchester. That was all they could afford.

'I remember one day, the coach – it was a bit on the old and creaking side – broke down when we were going to play a Saturday match at Crewe. We ended up getting changed on the supporters' coach and not reaching the ground until 2.30. We came back with them afterwards. For all that, they were fun days. I've got seven or eight friends from the time I played at Colchester. They are still in the game and we keep in touch. We were all very young then, and I suppose a bit naïve. We loved the game and were just happy to play it for a living. We didn't think about the lack of rewards.

'I've seen a lot of the world in three years at Arsenal. I've been to Australia, America, Bermuda, Portugal, Sweden and Spain. And that's while English clubs have been banned from playing in Europe. At Colchester, in six years, I went abroad once. It was to Majorca. The players all saved up £3 a week for an end of season trip.

'I recall that, to get a new pair of boots, your feet had to be showing through the old ones. You got a chitty and went to a local sports goods shop. First, you showed your old ones to the manager. If he thought they could still be repaired you would take them to the cobbler and come back with big leather strips covering the holes. You had one pair of rubbers, one pair with studs and a pair of trainers. They had to last you the season. Here at Arsenal the majority of the players wear sponsored boots.' Groves started the season with Puma and was negotiating a new deal with Lotto. 'Boots are no problem now. If I wanted, I could get two or three pairs a week.'

Groves, to his credit, has not forgotten his roots in League football. 'I still go on holiday with the lads who were with me at Colchester – Tony Adcock, Keith Day, Alec Chamberlain, Rudi Hedman, my brother-in-law Andy Farrell, who is now at Burnley, Ian Phillips and Mel Parkinson. All the wives get on well together and we are always on the phone to each other. I think it says a lot for the spirit we had at the club at the time. Having said that, I feel very much a part of Arsenal now. Not, say, to the extent David O'Leary has over recent years. To him, Highbury has been almost a second home. He is part of the folk lore here.

'But I'm starting to get some time in too. At Christmas I signed a new contract that will keep me at Arsenal until the end of the 1991 – 92 season. I like to believe it showed the boss had confidence in my ability to continue to do a job for Arsenal. I've never been a regular during the past three years, but only five or six of the present squad can claim that privilege. There are no guarantees for anyone at a club such as Arsenal. You can be the biggest star, but it doesn't mean your place is safe.

'There is also the reverse side. Another club can come in with a bid and the manager might think, "I only paid £75,000. That's a good offer. I'll sell." So it's nice to have a contract that gives you a little bit of security. I know I've always got to be looking over my shoulder. Complacency is something I cannot afford. Start to think you are part of the furniture, and your game can go to pieces very quickly.

'Certainly I'm a far better player than when I arrived at Highbury. How could I not be . . . training, playing and just watching the sort of players they have here. I just wish now I could have come to Arsenal when I was a bit younger. Tony Adams and David Rocastle, for example, had been here five years when I signed. They have been learning good habits and having the best coaching since they were kids. Bobby Roberts and Cyril Lea, at Colchester, were good coaches. But at a small club they could only do so much. Cyril Lea, in fact, did a brilliant job. There was never any money for him to spend on strengthening the team. I definitely don't remember him being able to buy a player. Later, they sold me – as well as Adcock, Chamberlain and Hedman and got about £400,000 for us. It was a tribute to the

job Cyril did there. We had all come through the ranks. From Colchester, Cyril went to Leicester and from there to coaching the youth team at West Bromwich Albion.

'Luck has a lot to do with what you achieve in football. I've seen players in the Fourth Division who would more than hold their own in the First. By the same token there are players in non-League who would do a better job than some of those you see in the Third and Fourth Divisions. It also comes down to a bit of desire . . . of deciding whether you want something badly enough. Stewart Houston always says you find your level in the game. Where you end up is where you deserve to be.'

Groves, in his early days at Arsenal, was a regular visitor to Colchester's games. 'I used to go to watch my old mates rather than the team,' he said. 'I've been back a couple of times this season but the feeling isn't the same. I find I'm watching a bunch of strangers. I get more pleasure going to see Burnley or Crystal Palace. I know players in their teams.'

His best friend at Highbury is Paul Merson, but Tony Adams is the player he most admires. 'He's a couple of years younger than me and he's won a League championship medal, been Young Player of the Year and is an England international. Not bad at twenty-two. All that hasn't affected him at all. He'll go down to his local pub, have a pint, and just be himself. I admire and respect that. His attitude is fantastic. I think if I had come here at seventeen and achieved what he has, it might have turned my head. Tony has displayed admirable maturity. He is just a nice bloke.'

Groves calls himself a 'day-to-day' person. 'I know all this will end one day. But I don't worry about the future. I think most footballers are the same. There are times when I get a bit depressed in training. Then I think to myself . . . "Here I am, running around to keep fit, having a great time doing it, and earning a good living. So why am I moaning." It's a fabulous career. When it ends, as it must do eventually, I'll have some fabulous memories.'

# 14
# IT'S OVER

*Steve Bould*

Nobody was saying as much for public consumption, but among themselves, the Arsenal players knew that was it. The championship they had won so gloriously the previous season would be going elsewhere this year.

It was 11 April and an unusually warm spring evening. Arsenal didn't need telling that if they could beat Aston Villa at Highbury and strugglers Charlton took three points off Liverpool on the other side of London, the title race would be blown wide open. Even with the game being screened live on ITV and with the BBC showing the FA Cup semi-final replay between Manchester United and Oldham, the prospect was attractive enough to draw a 30,060 crowd to Highbury. But five minutes

◄ **You won't get past me this way, says Arsenal's Steve Bould.**

from the end of a match Arsenal had dominated, full back Chris Price scored his first ever goal for Villa. It was enough to send Arsenal skidding to their second home defeat of the season. Liverpool won 4–0 at Selhurst Park, Arsenal were left 12 points behind the leaders, and it was impossible not to agree this was the end of the title road.

In the players' lounge afterwards the mood was subdued, but there was no air of obvious depression. It was as if Arsenal knew their cause had been lost before the eventful night. 'The boss wasn't happy about the result, but he was satisfied with the commitment,' said central defender Steve Bould. 'If we are to be realistic we were clutching at straws anyway. We had an outside chance – no more. Deep down I know the manager was as sick as the rest of us. But he said he was pleased with the way we had played, and he would tell people as much. My own feeling is that we are now left with mission impossible. It was the defeat that has, I suppose, seen us off. In the dressing room afterwards we all just sat there for 20 minutes feeling very dejected. Nobody said much. There was no criticism over the goal. One or two of the lads were questioning where Chris Price came from to get in a scoring position. The manager certainly didn't make an issue of it. John Lukic suggested David Platt might have been offside.'

The players' lounge is in the new building that houses the executive boxes at the Clock End of Highbury. Tables and chairs are dotted around a long room that has subdued lighting and plush carpets. A free bar at one end serves beer, spirits and soft drinks. Each player is allowed four guests. Prior to the 1989–90 season, the lounge used to lead off from the tunnel going down to the pitch. There were no windows and stars of the past used to claim they had seen bigger broom cupboards.

Bould, being unmarried and with his family living in Stoke, rarely uses his full allocation of players' lounge tickets. For the Villa game he had left a lounge ticket for an old school friend.

But the friend didn't linger. He left immediately after the final whistle. Bould didn't stay long himself. Arsenal might have lost, but this was still a night when the players had something to celebrate. Perry Groves' wife Mandy had presented him with a baby son, Lewis, and it had been agreed – win, lose or draw – they would go on from Highbury and wet the baby's head. The vast majority of professional footballers find it impossible, anyway, to get to sleep after a big match. The adrenalin is still flowing and they need to wind down.

Because of television's requirements the Villa match did not finish until 9.50 p.m. So it was after 11 p.m. when a group that included Groves, Bould, skipper Tony Adams, Brian Marwood, David Rocastle, Paul Merson, Michael Thomas, Kevin Campbell and Colin Pates kept a promise to attend a charity event for cancer research at a pub in Islington. From there, they went on to a club. It was just before 3 a.m. when Bould reached his home in St Albans.

For Bould, the season after Arsenal had been crowned champions did not start well. During the Makita tournament at Wembley he collected a groin injury. 'Originally, it was thought I would be fit for the Charity Shield a couple of weeks later. In fact it was five months before I played again. It seemed to be getting better when I went to the rehabilitation centre at Lilleshall. But the groin went again. I also did it a third time in training. Rest was to prove the only cure. But it was to be 30 December, when we lost 2–1 at Aston Villa, before I played my first full League game of the season. I hadn't even had a reserve match before that. I found myself in the squad but I didn't really expect to play. I obviously wasn't match fit. Missing the first part of the season means you are always struggling to catch up. I'm not the fittest player in the world anyway. I have to work hard to maintain a good level.'

When Bould first returned to the side, Arsenal used the sweeper system that had served them so well on the run-in to the championship. It was abandoned eight games later. On 27 February, Arsenal went to Charlton and it was back to 4-4-2. Bould stayed in the side partnering Tony Adams at the heart of the defence with popular David O'Leary on the substitutes' bench. 'When we first tried a sweeper system everything went fine,' said Bould. But it didn't suit everybody and one or two of the lads were not happy with it. This year we tried it, and there was a feeling it wasn't working. I know Tony Adams prefers 4-4-2.

'When you are winning games, nobody worries about the system. You can play 1-7-2 and it will be OK. You don't question it too much. On the run-in to the championship, using a sweeper, we were winning games and playing well. I was brought up playing 4-4-2. It is inevitable I will feel more comfortable playing that way.'

In fact, when Liverpool came to Highbury on 18 April, Kevin Richardson was ill and O'Leary was back in the side alongside Bould and Adams. 'I know it has been suggested we got a bit complacent after winning the League,' said Bould. 'To me, that's rubbish. I know I haven't lost my appetite for wanting to win things. I know that also applies to the other players here. Quite simply, we have found it hard to score goals this past season. A year ago we were pinching them from corners, free-kicks and every situation possible. This year the ball just hasn't gone in. Also, if we are totally honest with ourselves, we haven't played quite so well. Our away form has been shocking.'

You couldn't miss Bould in a crowd. At 6ft 3ins he is usually half-a-head above the rest. But Nottingham Forest did! He was there for several weeks as a fourteen-year-old, met Brian Clough and Peter Taylor, but was not given any encouragement to stay. 'I went back home to Stoke and thought I had missed my

---

▷ **Bould battles it out with one of the best strikers in the game – Everton's Graeme Sharp.**

chance. Stoke City picked me up when I was playing for the city's schools' side. I was happy to sign for them.'

It was in the summer of 1988 that Bould joined Arsenal. The fee of £390,000 was set by a transfer tribunal and he made his First Division début at Wimbledon on the opening day of the title-winning season.

'My contract at Stoke was up and I had heard some of the bigger clubs were after me. I thought to myself that if I didn't take the chance and move now I might miss the opportunity of a lifetime. I stuck my neck out and told Stoke I wouldn't be staying. It wasn't easy. I was a home town boy and I loved the place. They actually offered me a very attractive new deal, but leaving was still the best thing I ever did. Everton came in just before Arsenal, and I spoke to Collin Harvey. I was very impressed. It was really a spin of the coin job as to where I went. I felt, however, that the immediate future was with Arsenal. I reckoned Everton were rebuilding and it would take time. Arsenal I saw as a club where the whole thing was coming together and they were on the brink of doing great things.

'I also heard, the way you do on the grapevine, that Nottingham Forest were interested. As they had rejected me as a schoolboy I found that rather ironic. Stoke, I understood, were ready to offer me a contract covering the next four or five years and if nobody worthwhile had come in I would have been happy to stay. Mick Mills was manager at the time. Even when he realized I was on my way he didn't try to point me in any particular direction. But he wished me all the best whatever decision I made and I appreciated that.

'I spoke to Brian Talbot and to Alan Hudson, both former Arsenal players, as well as to Adrian Heath, who had gone to Everton from Stoke. Adrian told me to sign for Everton. When I see him now he still maintains I should

▷ **The long leg of Bould ends another moment of danger.**

have gone to Goodison. It was Alan and Brian who, I suppose, swung it. Huddy told me that when you walk through those doors at Highbury and go into the marble halls you are entering the greatest club in the world. It just hits you. There is nothing in football to beat it. I know he is still in love with the place. What Brian said was virtually the same. He said there is a magic feel about Arsenal. It is a very special club.

'There were those who told me I would find London a vast and unfriendly place after Stoke. I was warned that players from the North often find it hard to adapt. I was reminded that Charlie Nicholas didn't make it in the big city. I admit it hasn't been easy. London is indeed huge. Perry Groves, for instance, lives nearly 90 miles away from me. It helped that my girl friend Zoe came down from the Potteries to join me. The worst thing about those early days, before Zoe moved down and I bought a house at St Albans, was living in a hotel. Problems over completion meant I was there more than three months. It wasn't too bad at the start because pre-season training took most of the day and when that finished I was pretty exhausted. But it could still be a lonely existence. Actually adapting to life in London hasn't been difficult. The one thing I don't like is travelling on the Underground. I gather, however, it isn't something that is exclusive just to me.

'The major difference between Stoke City and Arsenal is the one you would expect: size and stature. At Arsenal, you come down Avenell Road towards the main entrance on a match day and it is difficult to get through the crowds. At Stoke, I would arrive at the ground before a game and there would be hardly anyone around. Here, the queues outside the turnstiles seem to be a mile long and the club shop as you pass by has lines of fans outside. For all that, I always found Stoke to be a well-

run club. They looked after the players and tried to do things right. It is tragic that they have been relegated.'

In the Potteries, the old-timers tell you Bould is the best centre half to come out of Stoke since the far-off days of Neil Franklin. Bould admits the First Division has been a testing experience. He rates Colin Clarke, of Queen's Park Rangers – now at Portsmouth – and Aston Villa's David Platt the best he has played against this past season.

'Clarke was superb in all the League and Cup games against us. I think all our defenders will agree with me. He gave us a lot of problems. Platt has lots of class. I believe he has a big future at the very highest level. Now, with Leeds being promoted, I expect I'll again come up against Lee Chapman. It is not a prospect I relish. He always seems to play well against me. Certainly he has when he was at Sheffield Wednesday. Not that Wednesday are one of my favourite sides. This year I scored an own goal at Hillsborough with my first kick of the game. It was after only 15 seconds. The manager hadn't got to his seat and we were a goal down. It didn't help that it was the only goal of the match.'

Bould accepts the discipline at Arsenal has to be tight. 'You are much more in the spotlight. You can't get away with anything. Step out of line, and somebody will find out. There is no hiding place.' Earlier in the season Bould, along with Paul Merson, was disciplined for an incident at a championship celebration function. 'We were loud that night. I didn't realize it at the time, but we were. While I think the incident was exaggerated, it is still something I regret. We were a bit boisterous, nothing more. There was a fight outside the hotel afterwards, but no Arsenal player was involved.'

Bould is more determined than ever to be up there with the best. He trained on his own throughout the summer. Which is proof enough that he means business this coming season.

◀ **Shall we dance together! Bould with Everton's Kevin Sheedy.**

# 15
# KEVIN'S WAY

*Kevin Richardson*

Kevin Richardson had been looking forward to the Everton game for weeks. Playing against his old club, a club for whom he retains the deepest affection, was still something special. It was in the days leading up to the 31 March Highbury encounter that Richardson first started feeling unwell. Stomach pains and a feeling of nausea were among the symptoms.

Inconsistency had damaged and eventually ended Arsenal's battle to hold on to their title. Lack of consistency was not a charge that could be levelled against Richardson. He will readily admit that his game does not have the silky touches of David Rocastle or the pinpoint passing of a Paul Davis fit and at his best. But there is a drive and purpose about Richardson

◀ **Kevin Richardson – his days at Arsenal were already numbered.**

that had made him invaluable to Arsenal's midfield prior to his summer move to Real Sociedad. George Graham bought him for a bargain £250,000 from Watford in August 1987. Geordie-born and bred, Richardson had spent seven years on Merseyside without ever reaching the point where it was possible for a manager to mark him down on the team-sheet as an automatic choice. At Arsenal, it was different. He usually made it difficult for manager Graham to leave him out.

It was 10 minutes from the end against Everton when Richardson accepted he could give no more. He was totally exhausted. 'I had been anything but right all week. Whatever it was, it just knocked me for six. During the game I was feeling really tired. I had to conserve my energy and take spells away from the action just to get my breath back. I found myself having a bit of a rest before I could go again. As the minutes ticked away I felt worse and worse. I knew the only answer was to get someone else on . . . someone who would have a fresh pair of legs. At the time we were winning 1 – 0. The important thing was to hold on for three points.

'I don't know how, but it seems I had picked up some sort of bug. After coming off against Everton I saw one of the club doctors, Leonard Sash. He gave me some tablets. I was hoping they would clear up the problem. They didn't. I just felt worse. I was going downhill all the time. I was doing some training and getting through, but it wasn't me. The boss knew before the Everton match that I had some sort of bug. I don't think he realized how bad it was. I don't think I did either. He obviously thought I could still do the job otherwise he wouldn't have picked me. Added to that, it was my old club, Everton. I wanted to play. I was digging deep for extra energy.

'That Sunday, immediately after the Everton game, I felt really rough – and it got worse. In the days that followed, Dr Sash was worried. So was I. He sent me to see a specialist and I was admitted to hospital in Paddington. I had

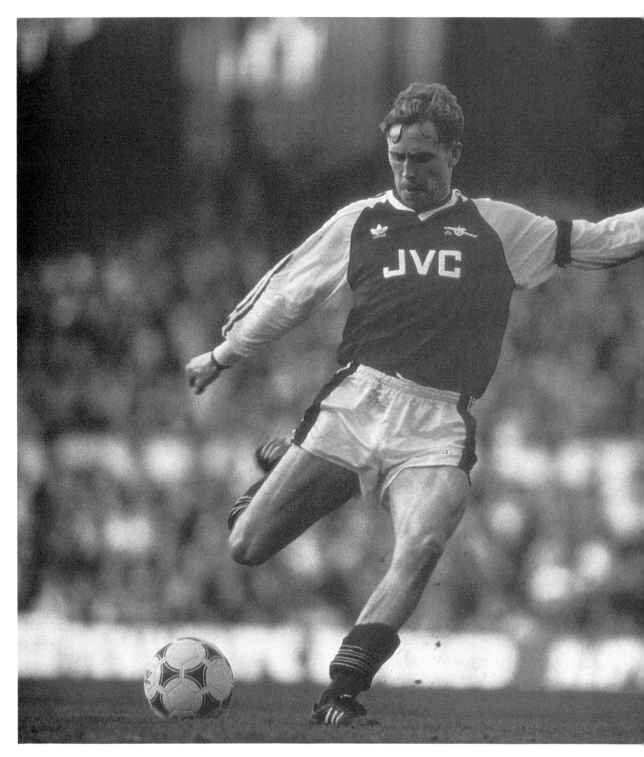

more tests than I care to remember. I was on a drip for four of the five days I was in there. I still don't know what the problem was. Doctors never tell you, do they? In fact, I understood it was some severe form of stomach virus. During the time I was ill I lost ten pounds in weight. I started to eat well once I came out of hospital. But I've been struggling to put the pounds back on. I'm looking to the summer, with no training and a holiday in Portugal, to get my weight back to what it was.

'They told me when I was discharged from hospital I would need a week away from football as a start towards getting back to my old self. It was suggested that I go for long walks and take it easy. Dr Sash suggested I went away. I took it as an opportunity to go up to Newcastle to see my parents. I enjoyed the rest. But not the way it came about. I had been an ever-present in the team up to the time the virus knocked me out. My most important target now is to be a 100 per cent fit and ready for the 1990–91 season in Spain.'

Richardson is no stranger to success. Before winning a League championship medal at Arsenal, he collected one with Everton. Winning medals with two different clubs makes him a member of a select band of players.

'When the season started I knew it was going to be a lot harder for all of us,' said Richardson. 'Remember, I had experienced a similar situation at Everton. With Arsenal, as it was at Everton, the ability and the determination to keep the title were there. But everyone would be trying extra hard to knock us down. I believe everyone at Highbury has learned from this season. I believe failure, and I suppose that's what it has to be when set against the year we won the title, will make all the good friends I have left behind better players. I also believe 1990–91 will be the season when Arsenal can win the championship again.

'In the year, during my time there, that Everton captured the First Division title, a lot

◀ **Eyes down as Richardson does it his way.**

▲ **Richardson, under pressure from Liverpool's Peter Beardsley, makes sure he is first.**

of the credit had to go to Howard Kendall as manager. He didn't worry about anything – certainly not our opponents. He just wanted the side to go out and play. He wanted us to express ourselves ... to play with a certain freedom. I think, when I was in the side, I was the only one who wasn't an international. He had a good blend of young and more experienced players.

'Off the field, too, there was a good mix of personalities. You had your serious ones, and those who could always make you laugh – in particular, Peter Reid and Andy Gray. Also, up

on Merseyside, everyone lived within easy reach of each other. You could call up any member of the side, and if they fancied a pint it would never take more than a few minutes to get together. I always believed that helped to build the fabulous team spirit we had at the time. Down here, because the players mainly live such distances from each other, it is difficult to do that sort of thing. You have your own friends, and they are often not in football.

'I was not a first team regular at Everton. I made no more than eighteen full appearances in the championship side, though I was on the substitutes' bench a lot. It was enough to guarantee me a medal. When we won the championship here at Arsenal, the boss did it

▲ **Richardson shrugs off a challenge from Southampton's Barry Horne.**

with a side that was tremendously well drilled as a unit. And again, the blend was perfect. George Graham knew his men, and he got the very best out of all of us. David Rocastle and I prove good examples. With Rocky, you are talking about a player who is great on the ball. A player with enviable skill. I haven't got that. But I could do things he couldn't. I'll run and I'll chase non-stop. We complemented each other. It is what team-work is all about. As a unit, we were definitely better than Everton. We had a more disciplined way of playing. It was a pleasure to be part of something that worked so smoothly.

'That it fell away this past season was a major disappointment to all of us. Teams definitely tried that bit harder against us. They made it hard for us to get into a rhythm. Possibly, they raised their game by 5 per cent and we were 5 per cent below what we were the previous season. It was enough to make the difference. Obviously, injuries to key players has also not helped. Injuries, when we won the championship, were, in the main, something that happened to someone else. It has not been easy for players coming in to the side, people like Martin Hayes.'

Richardson started the 1989–90 season by asking for a transfer. He says: 'It was a

contract situation that you get at all clubs. I'm twenty-seven and I was looking for a bit more. The boss made me an offer, adding two years to my old contract that had a year to run. It didn't affect my relationship with him or with Arsenal. I might have asked for a transfer, but I didn't see it as something that couldn't be resolved. I look at what we achieved under George Graham and it is a record of which we can all be proud. This is his team, playing his way, and you cannot argue or find fault with a manager who has won the First Division and taken the club to two Littlewoods Cup finals. He is an exceptionally good manager. I will always have good memories of my years at Arsenal.

'It is fair to say, however, that at the time I left Everton for Watford, I didn't want to move away from there either. They were another club on the up and up. But I wasn't a regular in the side and I had started to believe I never would be. I joined Watford because they were in the First Division and because I was impressed with Graham Taylor, the manager who had got them there. I played in every game during my first season at Vicarage Road. Then Mr Taylor left for Aston Villa and Dave Bassett arrived. Inevitably, he had his own ideas, his own plans for the players he wanted. After he joined the club we went on a pre-season tour and I figured in every game. We got back, and the first match of the season was against Wimbledon, his old side. I wasn't in the team. I wasn't even one of the substitutes. I found that a bit strange and I went in to see him. He was straight with me. In a nice way he said I was out. He didn't want me. He had plans and I wasn't part of them. But he was honest and up front. I was disappointed, deeply disappointed, but I was grateful too. At least I knew where I stood. He wasn't going to mess me about. Mr Bassett said he would let me go if he got the right offer. It was the start of the season and that at least gave me a chance.

'Before I joined Watford, Sheffield Wednesday

and Queen's Park Rangers had also come in for me. I only played two games in Watford's reserves after being made available before George Graham moved for me. I knew Sheffield Wednesday were in again and so were Charlton. I have always believed in my own ability. I will always believe I can do a job for someone. I know George Graham was well aware of what I could do for his side – from my time at Everton as much as anything else.

'I would not be telling the truth if I said I haven't missed the North. But not as much as I did when I first came South. As a professional footballer you have to go where you are wanted. And I don't kid myself. I have been lucky to play for Everton and then Arsenal. You are talking about two of the biggest clubs in British football – clubs that treat their players particularly well.

'George Graham has his own individual way of doing things, and I respect him. Howard Kendall is probably a bit more laid back. He will trade jokes with you. He mixes with the players. At Highbury, Mr Graham is very tight on discipline. If anything, he tends to keep his distance. But doing things their different ways they have both won the championship. They are two of the most successful managers of the last ten years. Mr Graham is a much more private person than Howard Kendall. Howard would have a drink with the lads. It isn't something George Graham would do. I don't know. Perhaps it is a good thing.

'At Arsenal, my best friend was Nigel Winterburn. I was living in Hemel Hempstead when he signed for Arsenal from Wimbledon. I invited him to drop in to our place for a cup of tea. His wife liked our house so much, they finished up buying it. We just moved 200 yards down the road.

'My best performance of the season was probably when we beat Sheffield Wednesday 5–0. Everything went right that day – for me as well as the team. It was a throwback to Arsenal's championship year . . . good football, good movement, good goals.'

◀ **Kevin puts his best foot forward.**

# 16
# DIXON'S
# DELIGHT

## *Lee Dixon*

As Arsenal's season, and the League championship with it, slid away, Lee Dixon's year got better and better. Throughout the campaign he had arguably been Arsenal's best and most consistent player. April, however, turned out to be the month that dwarfed the others. It started with Dixon winning the vote as top First Division right back in the Professional Footballers' Association annual poll. Then his wife Joanne presented him with a baby daughter, Olivia. They already had a son, Joshua, born six weeks before the move to Arsenal from Stoke. It finished with Dixon winning his first full England cap in the 4–2 win over Czechoslovakia. He admits the call to England's colours – considered overdue by many – was a surprise.

◀ **Lee Dixon – his outstanding season brought him his first full England cap.**

'We played Aston Villa at Highbury and Bobby Robson was quoted as saying he had come to watch me. But I was sure he hadn't come to see just me. After all, there was a big England contingent in our own line-up and Villa also had players in contention. I wasn't even playing in my customary role. Kevin Richardson was ill, so David O'Leary returned at right back and I was switched to the middle of the park. This was Wednesday, and I didn't realize the squads were being named the next day. Usually it is a Monday. This time it was a Thursday, less than 24 hours after Villa had more or less ended our title hopes.

'I taped the game and watched it when I got home that night. In some ways, I suppose it had taken some of the pressure off me, playing in midfield. It was later that I realized Mr Robson must have already made up his mind, anyway. At first I was a bit upset about finding myself in midfield for the Villa match. The season was drawing to a close and the England manager was on the point of making some very important decisions. Yet it might have actually worked in my favour. Mr Robson had seen Arsenal play several times and I like to think he knew what I could do at fullback. It could even have been another string to my bow – that I had played reasonably well against another World Cup contender, David Platt. Bobby Robson didn't say anything to me after the match. But then neither did George Graham.

'I actually picked up a bit of an injury and came in on the Thursday. I was sitting on the bench in the treatment room when the club's doctor John Crane, who is also the England doctor, came in. He said "Congratulations." I honestly didn't know what he was talking about. He said "You're in the England senior squad." I couldn't believe it. I thought he was joking. I said "If it isn't true I'm going to strangle you." It was no joke. It was a shock. But a nice one. I had expected to wait until the Monday before hearing anything. My injury, it was a jarred knee that had developed swelling, suddenly got dramatically better. It was not going to be a problem for Arsenal on the Saturday, but the news did my recovery no harm.'

There were League games against Crystal Palace, Liverpool and Luton to be played before Dixon's England dream would become reality. By the time he joined up with the international squad on Sunday, 22 April, Arsenal were very much ex-champions.

'David Rocastle was the only other Arsenal player in the squad. I think it was the poorest attendance by the club in a long time. In the immediate past, Tony Adams, Alan Smith, Michael Thomas and Nigel Winterburn had all been part of the England scene. I roomed with Rocky. It was good for me to have him there. He was able to give me little insights into what was expected. Trevor Steven was also in the squad. I knew him from my Burnley days. He was the number one star in the first team when I was in the reserves. He was in the side when I made my début there. It was a bit ironic. Here we were with history repeating itself at Wembley. I was playing for the first time for the full England team and Trevor was again in the side.

'When your football upbringing hasn't always been champagne, League titles and international caps, I suppose you will inevitably have a deeper appreciation of the good times. For all that, wherever I have been, no matter the club or the division, I have enjoyed myself. And I always felt I was learning. Back in 1983, when I was at Burnley, I regarded it as an honour just to get in the reserve side. At that time, when I was eighteen, Burnley were in the Second Division and the reserves were packed with good players. The first team was full of what, to me, were famous names – Martin Dobson, Billy Hamilton, Willie Donachie, Brian Flynn . . . there were quite a few internationals.

'I'm a Manchester boy and my clubs before Arsenal were all from around that area. You could say I was always able to work from home. I never needed to go and live in digs like some

of the younger players. My dad, Roy Dixon, was a former professional footballer. He was No. 2 goalkeeper to Bert Trautmann at Manchester City. He knew Gordon Clayton, who became youth team manager at Burnley, from his days in Manchester. He and my dad were good friends. I was messing around at Bolton on schoolboy forms and not getting anywhere. Dad mentioned it to Gordon, who said "Bring him down to Turf Moor." I was seventeen when I went to Burnley as a non-contract player for a year. I worked for my dad part-time and also went to college. I was studying A-level economics. I didn't finish the course. When I was eighteen, Burnley offered me terms. It was probably a good thing. I can't say my heart was in my studies. My father has his own business, supplying the butchers' trade. I suppose I could have fallen back on that, but a professional footballer was all I ever really wanted to be.

'Brian Miller was manager at the time I signed. Frank Casper was there as coach and Martin Dobson was still playing. Frank and Martin later went to Bury and it explains why they later became one of my clubs. I made my League début for Burnley after Brian Miller had been sacked and when Frank Casper was in charge as caretaker manager. There were three games left that season, Brian Laws, who is now at Nottingham Forest, was injured, and they stuck me in. The season finished with us getting relegated to the Third Division. Frank Casper got the sack and that summer the club appointed John Bond as manager. I was picked to play in the first two games of the new season. A week later I did my cartilage. I felt I was never really in favour anyway. When I was fit again, Mr Bond said things were not working out and he was giving me a "free". I was stunned. It is the sort of news that would come as a shock to any player. I had just turned nineteen. I had only been in the game 5 minutes, and here I was being told I wasn't wanted. It was the lowest point of my career.

▶ **Lee Dixon – sizing up the situation.**

'It would be totally accurate to say I didn't particularly get on with John Bond. He obviously didn't fancy what he saw in me. But then he never really gave me much of a chance. He made a decision. He was the manager and that was his right. People have said since then that he made a major mistake. I only know it was probably the best thing that could have happened to me. If I had stayed at Burnley things might not have worked out the way they have. I might have plodded along for a couple of seasons and then been given a "free". Who knows?

'I suppose what happened gave me a bit of a kick up the backside. I didn't have a club, yet all I wanted to be was a professional footballer. When John Bond arrived at Burnley he brought all his big names from previous clubs – Tommy Hutchison, Kevin Reeves, Dennis Tueart . . . players who had done it for him in the past. That went against the grain at Burnley. They were traditionalists, who kept things in the family and didn't go outside for first team players. They preferred to create the names. Now, all of a sudden, they had a manager bringing in players from outside who were earning good money. It was something the Burnley public wouldn't accept. The club didn't have much success and the fans blamed John Bond. They turned against him.

'I wasn't the only player he released. Brian Laws, who was a big favourite, was sold to Huddersfield for about £40,000. Others went, and he brought his own men in. He was the manager and he was doing things his way. But the biggest mistake was giving him the job in the first place. It wasn't the best decision the Burnley board ever made. They obviously thought a change and a new approach was needed. It just didn't work out. You only have to look at where the club are now to appreciate the decline that set in. It's a great shame. Even in these days of major city domination I regard

▶ **QPR's Andy Sinton fends off Michael Thomas – but he still has Lee Dixon to contend with.**

▲ **Dixon – getting the better of Paul Allen and the old enemy, Tottenham.**

Burnley as a big club. A club respected all over the country. It's sad to think that not so long ago they almost went out of the League.

'After Bond had given me that "free" Chester and Crewe came in. It was a straight choice. Not a great choice. I looked at the Fourth Division table and I couldn't find Chester. I should have started at the bottom, because that's where they were. Stuck right at the foot of the table. I joined them in the February. John McGrath, who was the manager, told me about his plans and of all the players he was going to sign. He did a brilliant job selling the club. So brilliant, I saw us going all the way to the First Division and then into Europe. We were going to go places together. The end of the season came and nothing had changed. We were still stuck at the bottom. We had to apply for re-election. Fortunately we were voted back in. It was before the days of the bottom club automatically dropping out of the League.

'That summer John McGrath did, in fact, sign a lot of new players. We improved. We finished third from bottom. I was in the side throughout the season. Again, we had to apply for re-election. I have to say I got on really well with big John. Results said that he wasn't the best manager in the world at that time. But he was great to be around and he was always completely honest with me. At the end of the day he gave me a lifeline from Burnley and I'll always be grateful to him for that. I was at Chester for a season and a half. After that second application to stay in the League I thought to myself "I can do better than this. I don't fancy doing the hat-trick." I went to the board and told them I wanted to leave. They said I could go if the money was right.

'Frank Casper, who was then at Bury, telephoned me and asked if I would like to go over there. I replied that I would love to join him. He was pleased with my reply, but reckoned there would be a bit of a problem with the fee. It looked as if they couldn't afford me. I asked Frank how much was I going to cost and he said it was £5,000. I thought – I'll pay it myself just to get away. But then Bury came back and said they had sorted it out. The actual fee was a compromise – £3,500.

'At the time, I was still living at home. I went to Bury and missed only one game in the season I spent there. I enjoyed myself. We had a good side and only just missed out on promotion. We finished outside the top four after being third at one stage. Frank and Martin Dobson had got things running well. It was a club where everyone seemed to enjoy themselves. I know I did.

'At the end of that season Stoke City came after me. For a while there had been whispers that they were interested. I had only signed a one-year contract at Bury. They offered me a new one and the transfer went to the independent tribunal to decide the fee. Stoke were only willing to offer about £30,000. Bury wanted £120,000 and I believe the deal was settled at £40,000. At one stage there was a suggestion Stoke were going to back out.

'I wasn't that long at Stoke – around a season and a half again. Arsenal is actually the longest I have ever been at one club! When I went to Stoke, Mick Mills was the manager, he's gone and now they are in the Third Division. Is it me? Most of the clubs I'm at seem to hit hard times! Stoke are another sad case. Again, they are a big club with tremendous potential. Steve Bould was at Stoke at the same time as me. We had a good side at one time. Sammy Chung was there as coach. He took a lot of pressure off the boss, rather in the way that Theo Foley did when he was at Arsenal. I liked Sammy. It was a happy club when I was there.

'I hadn't asked for a transfer at Stoke. But once more, there were whispers. I didn't think they could be right. After all, Micky Thomas was playing right back for Arsenal at the time, and playing very well. There had been talk in the *Sunday People* that I was moving, but nothing came of it. We played Arsenal in the Cup and it all appeared to have died down.

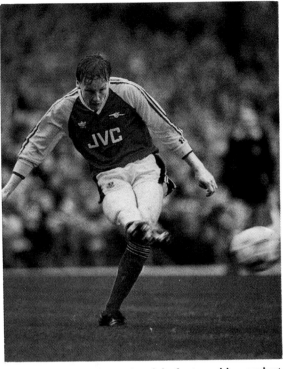

⬥ **Dixon gets his favourite right foot working against QPR in the FA Cup.**

'Later in the season, we met Leicester and George Graham was there. He talked to Mick Mills after the game, outside the dressing room at Filbert Street. The lads were joking that my new boss was waiting to take me away. Mick said they had talked and were sorting out the fee. The next day I went down to London for discussions. I understood the fee to be about £350,000. Money wasn't the reason I moved to Arsenal. It was more that I knew Arsenal were one of the biggest clubs in the game – if not the biggest.

'Everton had tried to buy me about six months before I moved to Arsenal, but their bid was rejected by the Stoke directors. Steve Bould had talks with Everton when he left Stoke, but I think I helped sway him towards Arsenal. Like me, I think he made the right decision. I told him how good, if a bit demanding, the training is, and how well the club look after their players.

133

'We won the championship and it was a long and varied road getting there. John McGrath sent me a nice letter when we captured the title. I didn't hear from John Bond! I wrote to John McGrath after he lost his job at Preston. I also wrote to Mick Mills when he was fired by Stoke.

'George Graham's commitment to his job and his determination to always do what he thinks is right are qualities that impress me tremendously. Everything he does is under the microscope, but George is his own man. He won't be swayed by the Press or anyone else. He always puts Arsenal Football Club first. Kenny Dalglish appears to be the same with Liverpool. It probably explains why they are both so successful. There was a time last year when I wasn't playing particularly well. George Graham dropped me. I wasn't pleased, but again it was a case of the boss putting the club first.'

Dixon has the sort of background that would appear to equip him ideally for an eventual move into management. He is still only twenty-six and that sort of move is a long way off. Yet he says: 'We get pressures as players, but nothing compared to what managers go through. A lot of it, I believe, is unfair. We get pressure from the manager. From the fans too. They get it from everywhere. But on a Saturday afternoon the manager can only be as good as his team. Right now, it is not a burden I feel I would want to carry. I have seen managers under strain – very much so. It tends to be a very lonely job. When you are winning, everyone wants to know you. But I have seen managers go home late at night looking as if they have spent the day at the local morgue. That sort of thing must have an effect on your family. I wouldn't like to arrive home looking like that. I think, just seeing the faces of the managers I have played for, even the successful ones, has made me realize they deserve every penny they get. Of course players, too,

◀ **Stoke's Carl Beeston finds they don't come any more determined than Lee Dixon.**

take it badly when the team has been beaten. You have lost a game, you have lost your bonus, you have possibly lost your position in the League. But players tend to get over a defeat quicker. The manager goes home and has got the whole weekend with the pressures that go with losing. He has got to talk to the Press as he tries to analyse what might have gone wrong. You see the joy that goes with success, but it is the agony I have seen on managers' faces in the privacy of the dressing room that sticks in my mind.

'There is nothing like being out there on the park, actively involved. Every manager is a frustrated player. It is why he does the job. You have to have a tremendous love of football to stay in the game as a manager. Managers, I think, are a breed apart. I don't think what it takes to be one is in me at the moment. But things could change. Who knows? You cross the line when you become a manager. You've got to change. I'm not sure it's worth it.'

Dixon shares the general disappointment at Highbury over Arsenal's failure to claim the championship for a second successive year. It is an echo of others when he says: 'What is more disappointing is that, with the potential we have at the club we could win the League every year. But we have been so inconsistent. The vast talent we have at the club has not fully expressed itself. I think we have let ourselves down. I know I wanted to win the championship just as much this year as I did a year ago. There is no reason why we shouldn't have been any less hungry for success. Look at Liverpool. They retain their appetite season after season.

'We've lacked a bit of the fire we had last year. We've also been without a lot of the luck that accompanied us in winning the title. There was talk, even before the season ended, that the boss was going to buy players. If you think too much about it, you can become a nervous wreck. What it should do is make us all more determined. It is nice to have a new face or two – as long as it isn't in your position! Hopefully, any signings will make us stronger.'

# 17
# NIGEL'S WINTER

*Nigel Winterburn*

Nigel Winterburn started the season believing Arsenal could repeat the championship success they had spent the summer celebrating. He ended it with his best pal, Kevin Richardson, heading for a new career in Spain at Real Sociedad, and accepting that a wind of change was blowing through Highbury.

'I'll miss Kevin,' said Winterburn. 'He lived just down the road from me in Hertfordshire. We used to room together on away trips and we were good friends. But we are all professional people, we have to accept that players will come and they will go. We are starting the 1990–91 season with some new faces and that can't be a bad thing.'

Winterburn is a laid-back character who never seems to let too much trouble him. There

◀ **Not this way, Pal! Liverpool's Peter Beardsley slides in to stop Nigel Winterburn.**

was a flowing confidence about his game in the championship year, that should have made his inclusion in England's World Cup squad little more than a formality. It didn't work out that way. He was one of a cluster of Arsenal stars who fell by the wayside. Winterburn admits: 'Personally, I didn't have a good season. I think there are other players in the club who would say the same thing about themselves. It is difficult to work out why.

'To this day I can't tell you why some of us saw our form fall away the way it did. Certainly, I didn't go into the season any differently. My own attitude of wanting to win every time I went out there hadn't changed. I feel sure every other player at the club had the same aim – believing we could be champions again. Perhaps the new season came too quickly for us. We were all on this high and perhaps we never came down out of the clouds.

'I didn't think we were ever in a challenging position or dominating the way we did when we won the title. In our championship year, the other clubs were chasing us after Christmas. This time, even when we were laying second or third we were pushing to make up points. The way we were playing we were never going to do it, something was missing. We failed, and it is history now. When the season started, I knew Liverpool would be the obvious danger. They always are. Every year throws up a surprise team. The previous season it was Millwall, this time it was Aston Villa. I didn't look on them as a real threat. In the end they deserved to finish runners-up to Liverpool.

'Certainly, the spirit in our dressing room was no different, we still had our characters. Brian Marwood, for instance, was still having a laugh and a joke. Heads didn't drop. In the end, I suppose, we were just not good enough.'

Winterburn joined Arsenal from Wimbledon in the early summer of 1987. The transfer fee was £350,000 – a bargain by anyone's standards. 'I found Arsenal a lot different to what I had known at Wimbledon. A heck of a lot different,' says Winterburn. 'For all that

you hear about Wimbledon, about the "Crazy Gang" and the way they do things, I think it has a lot to do with the difference in size and stature of the two clubs.

'At Wimbledon, before a game, anyone who had the slightest connection with the club seemed to be welcome in the dressing room. Everyone came in, directors, friends, family. An hour before a game you could have your uncle in there chatting away. Look at some of the results, and who could say it was wrong? At Arsenal, usually only the vice-chairman, David Dein, will look in and say "Hullo" and "Good Luck". Everyone at Wimbledon had a nickname, "Olly Beak" and "Bob Brush" – after having my hair cut very short – were among mine. I don't have much to do with the club now, but it is still the first result I look for. The team from my time there has been broken up, but it hasn't stopped them from being pretty successful.

'Some of the things we did in training at Wimbledon you would never see at Arsenal – or any other club. Yet they worked for us. For instance, we used to have games of American Football regularly on a Friday morning. There was a sectioned off part of the training ground where we would go and have fights. Everyone pitched in. Players would pin each other to the ground. Dave Bassett, who was then the manager, used to join in. Often, he was the instigator. It might seem hard to believe, but it was actually all good fun. It worked. It helped to create the terrific family atmosphere they had at Wimbledon. It relaxed us.

'I suppose I was one of the quieter ones. I was never a Vinny Jones or a John Kay. I tended to sit back a bit and play a spectator's role. Actually, I'm always a bit reserved until I get to know people.

'John Kay had this thick North East accent. None of us could understand him. He came to Wimbledon from Arsenal, with me, much later

◁ **QPR's Simon Barker is at full stretch, but Arsenal's Winterburn is up and away.**

▲ **Manchester United's Brian McClair seems determined not to let Winterburn beat him this time.**

making the journey in the opposite direction. He found it a different world, on the field, with Wimbledon's long ball game, as well as off it. I remember one day he got left out of a team in training. He went to ask why and was told it was because he was trying to play too much football. John said it wasn't his fault that he couldn't kick the ball as far as the rest of us.

'I didn't ask Wimbledon for a transfer. Dave Bassett had left the club and I had gone home to Coventry for the summer. I got a telephone call from Wimbledon asking me to return to Plough Lane. When I got there, I was told they had agreed a fee with Chelsea and I could go

and have talks. I saw John Hollins, who was then Chelsea's manager, but I didn't sign right away. I said I wanted a few days to think about it. While I was thinking they went out and signed Tony Dorigo. The next thing I knew, Arsenal had come in for me. I didn't take so long thinking it over this time!'

Winterburn recalls his early days at Highbury as being 'difficult'. He says: 'The boss told me when I signed that I would be a squad player, but I would get my chance, and when it came it would be up to me. Kenny Sansom was in the team at the time. I regarded him as a great player and I obviously accepted the

▷ **Nigel Winterburn – his season of high hope ended in disappointment.**

situation. Yet I always had the feeling that he might be leaving the club. As it turned out, it was sooner than I expected.

'I spent my first six months at Arsenal in the reserves. It wasn't an easy time for me – after all, I had known nothing but first team football at Wimbledon. OK, the gates for home games were not big, rarely more than five or six thousand, but suddenly I was going and playing in front of a few hundred. And that was on the good days. I look back, and I don't know how I did it. I had a bad time, motivating myself was difficult. I had never been in the reserves at Wimbledon. It all seemed so unreal. You couldn't even look at the League table on a Sunday morning to see where you were.

'The hardest time was at the end of the week when you knew all you had to look forward to was a game with the reserves. I thought it might be easier with Arsenal being such a big club, but it didn't work out that way. I just had to grit my teeth and press on in the hope of getting a break. Obviously, it crossed my mind that I had made a mistake. The boss had words with me on a couple of occasions. He encouraged me to keep plugging away. I think he realized I was finding it anything but easy. I hadn't gone to see him, he asked to see me.

'To start with, I wasn't playing at all well in the reserves, so he must have seen something was wrong. Suddenly things changed quite dramatically. My form picked up and I found myself in the first team. I made my Arsenal debut in my best position – left back. Kenny Sansom returned to the side and I was switched to right back. My right foot isn't my biggest asset. Basically, I can't use it. I do try, but I know I'm not as confident with it as I should be. Go through the four divisions, and there are not too many two-footed full backs. Most of them, though, can get away with using the weaker one when they have to. With me, it's usually in desperation.

◁ **'I'm too sharp for you,' Winterburn might say as he gets away from Everton's Graeme Sharp.**

143

'I more or less saw out the second half of that first season at right back, playing on the other side only a couple of times when Kenny was injured. I certainly didn't play consecutive games in that position. For all that, I enjoyed being in the team, but I wasn't particularly keen on the job I was being asked to do. Watford was probably my worst game in that period. I remember Rick Holden gave me a bad time. Generally, however, I seemed to get away with it.

'I always look back on the Littlewoods Cup Final, when we lost 3–2 to Luton, as the day I got found out. It was inevitable that it would happen. The result, combined with my own performance, spoiled a perfect afternoon. But I had got away with it for a long time. The following season, the championship year, I started at left back. Kenny was in the reserves, out of favour, I suppose. I didn't find that a difficult situation. I knew I had a job to do. I knew how well Kenny had served the club and the number of times he had been capped by England. But that wasn't my problem. My problem was to stay in the team. That was all I had to concentrate on. When I look back, I know I wasn't really worried about the shadow of Kenny in the background. I was in, he was out, and I knew that if I was playing well he would have to be going some to get me out.'

Birmingham City was Winterburn's first League club. He went there, eventually becoming an apprentice professional, after being spotted playing for Nuneaton Schoolboys by Don Dorman – one of football's legendary star finders. Jim Smith was manager.

'I did one year as an apprentice, then I signed as a full professional. I had been a pro for eighteen months when Ron Saunders arrived as the new manager. He had a massive clear-out. Twenty players went. I was one of them. I was playing in the reserves. We were regarded as surplus to requirements. It was the end of the season and he wanted to bring in his own players. I was eighteen. It came as a shock because I felt things had been going well. I had spoken to Jim Smith and he seemed very satisfied with my progress.

'What happened after that was a bit of a nightmare. It wasn't easy going home to my parents and telling them I wasn't wanted any more . . . that I had been released. I think it was an even bigger shock to them than it was to me. As it was the end of the season, it was a case of sitting around and just waiting. The worst part was not knowing what you were going to do if nothing came up. In the end I telephoned Jim Smith, who was then at Oxford. I trained pre-season with them for a couple of weeks. It was Jim who told me Wimbledon needed a left back and were interested. He told me to go there for a couple of weeks and see how things worked out. If they didn't, I could come back to Oxford. From nothing I now had two possibilities. Wimbledon were in the Third Division then. They had just been promoted. I went there – and stayed. I was more or less given a guarantee I would be in the first team. They didn't have anyone else.

'Coming to Arsenal from Wimbledon meant I had to learn a whole new style of play. But while we played it long from the back there, we were never told you had to hit everything 40 or 50 yards. If it was on to play short, we did. They were good days at Plough Lane. I wouldn't have missed them.'

There have been plenty of good days at Arsenal, too, for Winterburn. He has three years of his current contract to run. Winterburn, certainly, was not going to be affected by the wind of change.

◁ **Winterburn in action – following a different style of play than in his Wimbledon days.**

145

# 18
## ONE
## YEAR ON

*Michael Thomas*

The contrast for Michael Thomas could not have been more complete. Arsenal played their last League match of the season at Norwich, and Thomas found himself on the substitutes' bench. A year earlier, he had been a hero. Arsenal had gone to Liverpool needing to win by two clear goals to clinch their first championship in eighteen years, and Thomas had scored the second in spectacular fashion in the final minute, to give Arsenal a 2–0 win and the title. It was described, even by the less hysterical side of the mass media, as the most dramatic finale ever to a First Division championship race. What a difference a year was to make . . .

For the Liverpool game, Arsenal had travelled on the day of the match. To Norwich, for the

◀ **Michael Thomas – his season ended in an anti-climax.**

closing chapter to the 1989–90 campaign, they travelled overnight. The championship was gone, but manager George Graham stressed, with European football for English clubs a possibility in the season ahead, victory was important. It would enable Arsenal to hold on to third place.

'It was on Saturday morning, when the boss named the team, that I knew I wouldn't be in the starting line-up,' said Thomas. 'There had been no suggestion that I wouldn't get any further than being one of the subs. It came as a surprise. After all, this was the last game. I felt it was a bit late in the season to give me a rest. Certainly, when I went to bed on the Friday night I didn't think I wouldn't be in the side.'

George Graham had taken seventeen players to Norwich. 'There were rumours that Dave Rocastle could be back in the team. I also thought Kevin Richardson, who had recovered from illness, might play', said Thomas. 'I shared a room with Rocky, we usually share on away trips, but he didn't say anything. I expected him to play, but on the right wing, not in the centre of midfield. I couldn't understand it.

'But anyone who knows George Graham will tell you he doesn't broadcast his decisions. He keeps things to himself, and doesn't say anything to anyone. He always announces the team at his pre-match meeting. There are no explanations – before or afterwards.

'At Carrow Road I got on 20 minutes from the end. We were 2–1 down at the time. It was a tactical substitution – Paul Davis came off. My impression, sitting on the bench and afterwards, was that the boss wasn't too happy with some of the performances.'

Arsenal twice came from behind to collect a point from a 2–2 draw. Alan Smith scored both goals. But on the same final Saturday, Tottenham beat Southampton 2–1. It was enough to lift them above their North London rivals and into third place. Arsenal finished fourth.

In the first half of the season Thomas had been pleased with his form. In his own words he had a couple of so-so games after that and

was dropped when Arsenal played Wimbledon at Plough Lane on 13 January. 'I really didn't think I deserved to lose my place and it hit me hard. There was no explanation and it wasn't easy to take. As I've already said, you don't get explanations with George Graham, he drops you, and that's it. It's not worth arguing with him, you won't get anywhere.

'I went to the Wimbledon match, though to be truthful I felt more like going home, but I sat through it. I watched from the directors' box. All the Arsenal fans around me were asking why wasn't I playing? Had I been dropped? There wasn't a lot I could say. Rocky was also left out, though he was one of the substitutes on the bench. A week later we played Tottenham. I was back in for that one. It was the game that was to leave me with the injury to my right ankle that would present problems for the rest of the season.

'It happened in the final minute. I received the ball from Paul Davis and was moving away when David Howells came in with a full-blooded challenge from the side. I wasn't too pleased at the time, in fact, I wasn't happy at all. There were a lot of important games coming up – involving England as well as Arsenal. I had been hoping for an injury-free season – what with the World Cup at the end of it. Howells' tackle put paid to that.

'We played Queen's Park Rangers in the FA Cup at the end of January and I was still having problems. The boss didn't want to risk me for the whole game and I was on the bench. I played in the replay following the goalless draw at Highbury. But it was a mistake, I wasn't fit. I hadn't been able to train properly – most of my time was taken up with treatment – and I rushed back too early. I missed a 1–0 defeat at Sheffield Wednesday, then later, I played in a midweek reserve fixture at Oxford and came back for the goalless draw at Charlton.

'There is no question that my form suffered because of the injury. I couldn't do a lot of

**Thomas thunders in as Grobbelaar goes down.**

▲ **It's Thomas the Tank as a challenge from Derby's Geriant Williams is beaten off.**

things that were normally no problem. I couldn't, without feeling pain, kick the ball head-on. I couldn't fully stretch my leg. The slightest contact with my ankle and I was down, usually feeling as if I had been kicked by a horse. Even in training I had to restrict my shooting, and I was having treatment for much of the time. We had heavy injury problems: Paul Davis was out, so was Siggi Jonsson. We didn't have anybody else to bring in, so it was a case of having to play.

'At the start of every season, I set myself targets. When the 1989–90 season opened, my aim was to go with England to the World Cup. I wouldn't say I expected to be one of the chosen twenty-two, but I knew that if my form held, I would have a good chance. It was not to be. I was in the England squad, and among the substitutes, when Brazil came to Wembley at the end of March. Bobby Robson told me before the game that I wouldn't be playing because of my ankle. The injury ruined my season. It couldn't have happened at a worse time. It probably wrecked my chances of going to the World Cup Finals.

'David Howells didn't apologize afterwards for his tackle in that Tottenham game, but I'm not holding any grudge. What he did wasn't deliberate, he isn't that type of player. I'm afraid it was the sort of thing that will always happen in football.

'I suppose it was around the time of the Brazil match that I realized my chances of making the World Cup were disappearing. Because of my ankle, I hadn't even expected to be in the squad for that game. I just wasn't fit. It was the last contact I had with Bobby Robson in his time as England manager. There was no word from him between then and the announce-

▲ **Michael Thomas's greatest moment . . . the goal that won the League Championship.**

ment of the squad for Italy. I know people say I'm young, and there will be other World Cups, but right now, four years seems a heck of a long way away.

'George Graham has done a lot for me. We have our differences. We don't always see eye to eye. But overall, he leaves me alone, I leave him alone. I think it isn't a bad thing to keep your distance from the boss whoever he is and whatever the club. Doing your job the right way, whether you are manager or player, is what matters. At Arsenal, I think we do it the right way.

'That Liverpool game was so different to Norwich. The confidence among the players, and at the club, was unbelievable. The atmosphere in the days leading up to the match was brilliant. There was a terrific camaraderie in training. We were playing five-a-sides all the time – something we never normally do. In fact, everything we usually did in training was bombed out of the window. The mood was so relaxed, there was no tension. It was remarkable when you consider the importance of the game we were facing.

'On the day of the match, we left the training ground at London Colney at 8 a.m. We got to the hotel at mid-day and I went straight to bed. For five hours I slept like a log. When I woke up, I felt good. Later, when my goal went in, I didn't know how long there was to go. There were no signals from the bench and I thought there must be 15 to 20 minutes left, I didn't realize that was it. I've got a video of the game, but I never watch it. If I did, I would panic – thinking Liverpool were going to catch me before I could put the ball in the net.

'That season has gone anyway. I've got to look to the future, not the past. Friends tell me I have gone down in history for that goal, but

that's what it is . . . history. I've got a library of videos of Arsenal games, which I never look at. Maybe in twenty years time I'll get them all out to remind myself of what it was like.

'I remember I celebrated that goal at Liverpool from the moment the final whistle went. I got a bit drunk on the journey home to London. I wasn't alone. The following morning, after sleeping for a couple of hours, I went out and there seemed to be fans in Arsenal shirts, bobble hats and scarves everywhere. People who weren't even Arsenal supporters recognized me. I suppose that is what television does.

'I've got my championship medal, but it is never out on show. I have a display cabinet with all the caps I've won at different levels, but the medal is kept safely elsewhere.'

Thomas, Lambeth-born, built like a slimline mini tank, and only twenty-three when the 1989–90 season ended, came to prominence at Arsenal as a full back. 'I switched when Steve Williams was suspended for a Cup game against Everton. We had gone to Marbella and were training out there. The next thing I knew, the boss was telling me I was going to be in midfield.

'I wouldn't be telling the truth if I said that Liverpool game hasn't affected my life. People who talk to me about football always bring up the goal I scored that night. But I want to be known for more than that. I got loads of letters afterwards. Some of them were very touching. Fans wrote to say that what I did had brightened their lives. That the League championship returning to Highbury was the realization of a dream. I received countless invitations to attend various functions. I declined many of them, I'm not one for the spotlight.' Months later, the shirt Thomas wore that night raised £10,000 at a charity auction.

'The future? I've got two years to go on my contract. What happens after that we'll have to wait and see. Playing abroad one day certainly appeals to me. I'm a great admirer of the sort of

◁ **Thomas – about to do a football version of the limbo dance?**

football you see in Italy.

'I was in my last year at school when I signed for Arsenal. I also had the chance to go to Chelsea. I sat down with a good friend, Brian Johncock, who was my maths and football teacher at the time, and we weighed up the things for and against each club. What swayed me towards Arsenal was the stability of the club. Chelsea, in those days, seemed really rocky. They were changing managers almost every year. You never knew who was going to be in charge. One manager might sign you, but the next one would inherit you and perhaps not rate you at all. Arsenal, even then, struck me as being much more stable. Terry Neill was manager when I signed. Then Don Howe took over. But at least they kept it in the family!

'When I was a kid I loved watching attractive football – teams whose passing and technique were above the average. At that time, for me, Tottenham played the most fluent football in London. Foreign football I called it. I used to go and watch them all the time. Glenn Hoddle was my idol. He was an artist . . . a genius in my eyes. Ossie Ardiles and Ricky Villa were there too, great players, both of them. I always felt Villa never got the recognition he deserved.

'I was fourteen when I made up my mind to write to Tottenham for a trial. I actually went to train there a couple of times. Keith Burkinshaw was manager, with Robbie Stepney and John Moncur coaching the kids. Before I signed for Arsenal, they asked me to go back there again, but I had by then made my decision.

'Where did it go wrong this past season? It was probably a combination of things. We were champions, and teams were trying that extra bit harder to beat us. It meant additional pressure and we found it difficult to cope. Also, our strikers were not scoring. Neither were the midfield men. That made it doubly hard for the back four. At first, certainly up to November, I was cracking in the goals myself, then they dried up and I was able to understand how the strikers felt. Now, it's another season. We've got things to prove.'

# 19

# THE

# VERDICT

The season was in its final days. George Graham sat in the small office he occupied to the left of Highbury's marble halls. It was a time for reflection.

When a manager is not on the training ground, his office is a refuge where he can take a break from working with players, somewhere he can see them when they have a problem, answer his mail, plan his diary, talk to the media and relax with close friends after a match. They vary in opulence. At Arsenal, the manager's office – certainly before the club's major rebuilding scheme got under way – was not large. It was not opulent. It was wood-panelled and dominated by the desk behind which Graham, and Bertie Mee before him, planned League and Cup triumphs. Striking

◀ **Where did it go? George Graham could be reflecting on a League Championship that left Arsenal.**

sketches of the glory game adorned the walls, along with the usual fixture lists and board that shows the club's playing staff at every level, from first team squad to young hopefuls. With half-a-dozen in the room it always seemed crowded. Yet, being Arsenal, you could almost reach out and touch the tradition. And it was plush enough in its own cramped way.

This day, the manager who has brought the fans and the honours back to one of football's most famous clubs was in a contemplative mood. He accepted that a season promising so much after the dramatic championship success of the year before was ending with little to show for it. The glory has gone elsewhere. He says:

'The first word that comes to my mind in summing up the season . . . disappointment. It has been an inconsistent year for so many clubs – not just Arsenal. The possible exception are Aston Villa, because they didn't really expect to be up there as title challengers. I don't think even Liverpool have maintained their usual standards. Unfortunately for us and one or two others, the standards they have set are better than those of anyone else. In our case, instead of making winning the championship a platform for further success we let our standards drop.

'Anyone and everyone can have their opinion of the players, of the management, of the buying and selling and of the system we played. The thing is we still had the basic team and the basic squad that had taken the title the previous season. I would have to say that more than half the team fell below the standards they set in winning the championship. Half the team did not play anywhere near as well – consistently over the season that is – as they did when we won the title. Some of them were very fortunate to be included in an Arsenal team on the form they showed at times.

'One of the things we had in the championship year, that Liverpool always seem to have, was a hunger and a desire. Rediscovering that hunger and desire must be our priority in 1990–91. There was never, in my opinion, a

155

question mark against the talent we have in the club . . . though you can always improve the odd one or two.

'We have a young team that we would have expected to get better. Instead of getting better, we have actually gone backwards. I am hoping the lesson has been learned. This past year I found myself working twice as hard at motivating players before games and at half-time than I did in the previous three years.

'There are, of course, always plusses. Tony Adams is an excellent example. He took a lot of criticism in our championship year. But he came through it and I believe is a better player for the experience. He had a fine season. Like everyone, he can still improve certain aspects of his game. If he works on them, I'm sure he will. Lee Dixon, like Tony, can look back on a fine season. They must be the front runners for the title of Arsenal's best player.

'Looking back, there is nothing, really, I would have done differently – apart from getting one or two new players! But who do you buy if the ones you want are not available? I'm not the sort of manager who believes you should stick with a squad just because they won the championship. But I honestly believed the players we had, being so young, would improve. In a lot of cases the reverse happened. That wasn't good enough. We were champions and it was inevitable that other teams would be trying that much harder against us.'

In the end, Arsenal had to settle for fourth place – a formidable enough achievement. It was only on the final day of the season that Tottenham inched above them to claim a top three spot.

The Cups were a disappointment. The Littlewoods Cup, a competition in which Arsenal had reached two finals under Graham's inspired management, looked promising after Plymouth had been outclassed and then Liverpool beaten by an Alan Smith goal in the third round. But then Arsenal fell where so many others flopped this past season – on Oldham Athletic's Boundary Park plastic. In the FA Cup, Arsenal got past Stoke City comfortably enough in the third round, only to follow that by going under to former manager Don Howe in a replay at Queen's Park Rangers.

At home, Arsenal had seemed almost invincible. It was 17 March before they suffered defeat at Highbury – Chelsea coming across from West London to win 1–0. The previous season, Arsenal's ability to triumph on foreign soil had been a principal factor behind their championship success. This time, the team's away form was their downfall. Just four games were won away from Highbury. Only Everton, Manchester City and Luton, outside of the relegated clubs, managed fewer away wins.

There were, of course, injuries – of the sort that had not afflicted Arsenal a year earlier. Paul Davis missed most of the season. Brian Marwood missed much of it. And a troublesome back injury saw new signing Siggi Jonsson sidelined for a long time. Michael Thomas and David Rocastle, so dynamic in the championship season, suffered inexplicable losses of form.

And the goals dried up. Arsenal managed only fifty-four in the League. It was never going to be enough. But Kevin Campbell showed the potential to suggest he can be a major force in a new season, while Paul Merson, if his attitude is right, can finally make the breakthrough to be a forward of outstanding quality.

Manager George Graham, hungry as ever for continued success, knew the fresh players he wanted even before the season had ended. He said goodbye to 1989–90 with the words: 'We won't be left behind when it comes to challenging again for the title.' The rest of the First Division had better look out!

# EPILOGUE

It was more than the end of a season, it was the end of an era. The team had failed to keep the title. It was time for changes.

John Lukic had lived all year with the shadow of David Seaman in his goalmouth. The last echo of the final whistle had barely died when George Graham did the inevitable and paid £1.3 million for the QPR goalkeeper. Seaman will be happy if his time at Highbury is as successful as the spell enjoyed by Lukic. The new goalkeeper's contract had only just been filed away when Lukic left for Leeds for £1 million – and that was good business, with Lukic three years older than Seaman.

Lukic headed for Elland Road saying, 'I don't think I let anyone down in my time at Arsenal. In the end, though, it is others who must make that judgement. The supporters at Highbury were always marvellous to me. I will never forget them – or the reception they gave me at the end of our final home game of the season against Southampton. I can only hope I get a similar response from the Leeds public.'

Two players who had been restless throughout the season soon followed Lukic on the transfer trail. Kevin Richardson went to Real Sociedad for £750,000, and again Arsenal were able to argue they had got the better of the deal considering he had been bought from Watford for £250,000.

Martin Hayes had been a Celtic target for more than a year. At the end of May he became their player for a fee of £650,000. Hayes, with his pace and power, had looked a potential star in his early days with Arsenal. He never quite made it. 'It was the right time for me to move on,' said Hayes. He went with the genuine good wishes of everyone at Highbury.

Brian Marwood asked to go and that summer, there were times when the comings and goings made Arsenal seem busier than Victoria Station during rush hour. Andy Linighan signed from Norwich for £1.3 million and it became clear that wouldn't be the end of either the arrivals or the departures.

Perhaps the most surprising farewell was made by Theo Foley, Graham's assistant manager and right-hand man at Arsenal and at Millwall before. Foley left to manage Northampton, a club where he had enjoyed great success as a player in former years. 'I've got a chance of going back there and doing something,' he said. 'I had four great years at Arsenal and I wouldn't have missed a minute of it. I've got some fantastic memories. But the time has come to go my own way.'

The season had started with Arsenal looking certain to be heavily represented at the World Cup Finals. Tony Adams, Lee Dixon, Nigel Winterburn, David Rocastle, Paul Davis, Alan Smith and Brian Marwood had all, at some time, hoped to make it with England to Italy. In the end, none of them did. Hardest hit were Adams, Rocastle and Smith, asked to fall out at the last possible moment when England manager Bobby Robson cut his training squad by four to the final twenty-two.

Ironically, the only Arsenal player in Italy with England was David Seaman, and his World Cup was cut short by injury. David O'Leary also went to the finals, with the Republic of Ireland, and scored a memorable decider in a penalty play-off against Romania.

The redevelopment of Highbury following the Taylor Report, began as the season ended. The club and players' representative Jerome Anderson also reached agreement for the players to be much more closely involved with the local community through personal appearances, signing sessions and get-togethers. 'The fans will get closer to the players and it has to be good for the game,' said Anderson.

A new season was just over the horizon. A new, refreshed Arsenal were ready to meet it.

# ROLL CALL

When the season ended, the Arsenal playing staff stood at thirty-six professionals and fifteen Youth Training Scheme youngsters. Of those thirty-six professionals, six were told their careers at Highbury were over. They were given free transfers. These thirty players were under contract:

| | |
|---|---|
| Tony Adams | John Lukic[2] |
| Kwame Ampadu | Alan Miller |
| Steve Bould | Stephen Morrow |
| Andrew Cole | Brian Marwood |
| James Carstairs | Paul Merson |
| Kevin Campbell | Craig McKernon |
| Gus Caesar | Gary McKeown |
| Lee Dixon | David O'Leary |
| Paul Davis | Colin Pates |
| Perry Groves | David Rocastle |
| Neil Heany | Kevin Richardson[3] |
| David Hillier | Alan Smith |
| Charlie Hartfield | Pat Scully |
| Martin Hayes[1] | Michael Thomas |
| Siggi Jonsson | Nigel Winterburn |

(Now at [1]Celtic, [2]Leeds United, [3]Real Sociedad)

The six who went – they were told three weeks before the end of the season and their names circulated to every Football League club – were:

| | |
|---|---|
| Dino Connolly | Al James Hannigan |
| Lee Francis | Raymond Lee |
| Colin Hoyle | Andrew Mockler |

These were the fifteen YTS boys:

| | |
|---|---|
| John Bacon | Kevin Fowler |
| Steve Clements | Craig Gaunt |
| Paul Dickov | Ty Gooden |
| Richard Faulkner | Matthew Joseph |
| Mark Flatts | Scott Marshall |
| Ray Parlour | James Will |
| Danny Warden | Stuart Young |
| Kenny Webster | |

But a football club is more than just the players. At Arsenal, last season, there were manager George Graham, his assistant Theo Foley, and the coaches – Stewart Houston (reserves) and Pat Rice (youth). When the 1990–91 season opened, Foley had moved to Northampton Town as manager, with Houston promoted to first team coach.

Steve Burtenshaw (chief) and Terry Murphy head an army of scouts. Gary Lewin is physiotherapist, Tony Donnelly the kit manager, Vic Akers is assistant kit manager and Ethel Donnelly does the laundry.

Ken Friar is managing director and secretary. David Miles, one of several long-service employees, joined Arsenal straight from school in 1971. A former box office manager, he has been assistant secretary and right-hand man to Ken Friar since 1980 and is regarded as one of football's brightest young administrators.

Also on the Highbury staff are:

Box Office: Sue Compton, Iain Cook, Lynne Chaney, Toby Keswick.
Secretarial: Sheila Horne, Shelley Alger, Joanne Cawdery.
Junior Gunners: Debbie Wakeford, Sue Connelly.
Accounts: Paul Farmer, Brett Alger.
Gunners Shop: Simon Birch, Sue Williams, Tony Heather, Alison Grubb.
Travel Club: Paul Johnson.
Commercial and Marketing: Phil Carling, John Hazell, Julie Page.
Community Programme: Alan Sefton, Bill Graves, Mary Sampson, Freddie Hudson, Mark Antoniewicz.
Ground Staff: John Beattie, Bill James, Willie Fennell, Pat Galligan, John Callaghan, Pat O'Connor, Wally Pearce, Dick Walsh, Arthur Young, John Crow, Maureen Byrne, Wayne Phillipson, Billy O'Connor, Steve Braddock, Eve Bradshaw.

## THE ARSENAL RECORD FOR 1989–90 SENIOR TEAM (EXCLUDING FRIENDLY MATCHES)

| Date | Competition | Opponents | Venue | Score | Crowd | Lukic | Dixon | Winterburn | Thomas | O'Leary | Adams | Rocastle | Richardson | Smith | Bould | Merson | Substitutes | Goalscorers |
|---|---|---|---|---|---|---|---|---|---|---|---|---|---|---|---|---|---|---|
| 29 July | Makita International Tournament | VFC Porto | WS | W 1-0 | 20,374 | ‥ | ‥ | ‥ | ‥ | ‥ | ‥ | ‥ | ‥ | ‥ | ‥ | ‥ | Hayes (70 min), Campbell (86 min) | Own goal |
| 30 July | Makita International Tournament | Liverpool | WS | W 1-0 | 23,026 | ‥ | ‥ | ‥ | ‥ | ‥ | ‥ | ‥ | ‥ | ‥ | Caesar | ‥ | Caesar (H/T), Hayes (88) | Bould |
| 6 Aug | Zenith Challenge Match | Independiente of Argentina | M | W 2-1 | 5,000 | ‥ | ‥ | Morrow | ‥ | ‥ | ‥ | ‥ | ‥ | ‥ | Caesar | ‥ | | Rocastle (2) |
| 12 Aug | FA Charity Shield | Liverpool | WS | L 0-1 | 63,149 | ‥ | ‥ | Winterburn | ‥ | ‥ | ‥ | ‥ | ‥ | ‥ | ‥ | ‥ | Marwood (59), Quinn (79) | |
| 19 Aug | Football League | Manchester U | A | L 4-1 | 47,245 | ‥ | ‥ | ‥ | ‥ | ‥ | ‥ | ‥ | ‥ | ‥ | ‥ | Marwood | Caesar (17), Groves (80) | Rocastle |
| 22 Aug | Football League | Coventry C | H | W 2-0 | 33,886 | ‥ | ‥ | ‥ | ‥ | ‥ | ‥ | ‥ | ‥ | ‥ | ‥ | ‥ | Groves (84) | Thomas, Marwood |
| 26 Aug | Football League | Wimbledon | H | D 0-0 | 32,279 | ‥ | ‥ | ‥ | ‥ | ‥ | ‥ | ‥ | ‥ | ‥ | ‥ | ‥ | Groves (76) | |
| 9 Sept | Football League | Sheffield W | H | W 5-0 | 30,058 | ‥ | ‥ | ‥ | ‥ | ‥ | ‥ | ‥ | ‥ | ‥ | ‥ | ‥ | | Thomas, Adams, Smith, Merson, Marwood |
| 16 Sept | Football League | Nottingham F | A | W 1-2 | 22,216 | ‥ | ‥ | ‥ | ‥ | ‥ | ‥ | ‥ | ‥ | ‥ | ‥ | ‥ | Groves (82) | Merson, Marwood |
| 19 Sept | League Cup 2nd Rd | Plymouth A | H | W 2-0 | 26,865 | ‥ | ‥ | ‥ | ‥ | ‥ | ‥ | ‥ | ‥ | ‥ | ‥ | ‥ | Groves (62) | Rocastle, Smith |
| 23 Sept | Football League | Charlton A | H | W 1-0 | 34,583 | ‥ | ‥ | ‥ | ‥ | ‥ | ‥ | ‥ | ‥ | ‥ | ‥ | ‥ | Groves (80) | Marwood |
| 30 Sept | Football League | Chelsea | A | D 0-0 | 31,833 | ‥ | ‥ | ‥ | ‥ | ‥ | ‥ | ‥ | Groves | ‥ | ‥ | Hayes | Merson (76) | |
| 3 Oct | League Cup 2nd Rd | Plymouth A | A | W 1-6 | 17,360 | ‥ | ‥ | ‥ | ‥ | ‥ | ‥ | ‥ | ‥ | ‥ | ‥ | ‥ | Merson (74), Caesar (85) | Thomas (3), Rocastle, Smith, Groves |
| 14 Oct | Football League | Manchester C | H | W 4-0 | 40,414 | ‥ | ‥ | ‥ | ‥ | ‥ | ‥ | ‥ | ‥ | ‥ | ‥ | Marwood | Merson (73), Jonsson (73) | Merson, Marwood |
| 18 Oct | Football League | Tottenham H | A | L 2-1 | 33,944 | ‥ | ‥ | ‥ | ‥ | ‥ | ‥ | ‥ | ‥ | ‥ | ‥ | Hayes | Merson (68), Jonsson (75) | Thomas |
| 21 Oct | Football League | Everton | A | L 3-0 | 32,917 | ‥ | ‥ | ‥ | ‥ | ‥ | ‥ | ‥ | Quinn | ‥ | Merson | ‥ | Smith (76) | Smith |
| 25 Oct | League Cup 3rd Rd | Liverpool | H | W 1-0 | 40,814 | ‥ | ‥ | ‥ | ‥ | ‥ | ‥ | ‥ | Smith | ‥ | ‥ | Smith | Smith (65) | Smith |
| 28 Oct | Football League | Derby Co | H | D 1-1 | 33,189 | ‥ | ‥ | ‥ | ‥ | ‥ | ‥ | ‥ | Quinn | ‥ | ‥ | Merson | Campbell (72), Jonsson (72) | |
| 4 Nov | Football League | Norwich C | H | W 4-3 | 35,338 | ‥ | ‥ | ‥ | ‥ | ‥ | ‥ | ‥ | ‥ | ‥ | ‥ | ‥ | Groves (81) | Dixon (2), O'Leary, Quinn |
| 11 Nov | Football League | Millwall | A | W 1-2 | 17,265 | ‥ | ‥ | ‥ | ‥ | ‥ | ‥ | ‥ | ‥ | ‥ | ‥ | Marwood | Groves (70) | Thomas, Quinn |
| 18 Nov | Football League | QPR | H | W 3-0 | 38,236 | ‥ | ‥ | ‥ | ‥ | ‥ | ‥ | ‥ | ‥ | ‥ | ‥ | Jonsson | Groves (70), Jonsson (84) | Dixon, Smith, Jonsson |
| 22 Nov | League Cup 4th Rd | Oldham A | A | L 3-1 | 14,924 | ‥ | ‥ | ‥ | ‥ | ‥ | ‥ | ‥ | ‥ | ‥ | ‥ | Groves | Groves (75) | Quinn |
| 26 Nov | Football League | Liverpool | A | L 2-1 | 39,983 | ‥ | ‥ | ‥ | ‥ | ‥ | ‥ | ‥ | ‥ | ‥ | ‥ | Marwood | Hayes (71), Jonsson (72) | Smith |
| 3 Dec | Football League | Manchester U | H | W 1-0 | 34,484 | ‥ | ‥ | ‥ | ‥ | ‥ | ‥ | ‥ | ‥ | ‥ | Groves | Merson | Merson (70) | Groves |
| 9 Dec | Football League | Coventry C | A | W 0-1 | 16,255 | ‥ | ‥ | ‥ | ‥ | ‥ | ‥ | ‥ | ‥ | ‥ | ‥ | ‥ | Merson (70) | Smith |
| 16 Dec | Football League | Luton T | H | W 3-2 | 28,761 | ‥ | ‥ | ‥ | ‥ | ‥ | ‥ | ‥ | ‥ | ‥ | ‥ | Marwood | Merson (29) | Smith, Marwood, Merson |
| 19 Dec | Zenith Challenge Match | Glasgow R | G | W 1-2 | 31,118 | ‥ | ‥ | ‥ | Davis | ‥ | ‥ | ‥ | Quinn | ‥ | Merson | ‥ | Groves (25), Caesar (30), Hayes (88) | Davis, Quinn |
| 26 Dec | Football League | Southampton | A | L 1-0 | 20,229 | ‥ | ‥ | ‥ | ‥ | ‥ | ‥ | ‥ | ‥ | ‥ | ‥ | ‥ | Davis (66), Groves (74) | |
| 30 Dec | Football League | Aston Villa | A | L 2-1 | 40,665 | ‥ | ‥ | ‥ | Thomas | ‥ | ‥ | Groves | ‥ | ‥ | Bould | ‥ | Rocastle (75) | Adams |
| 1 Jan | Football League | Crystal Palace | H | W 4-1 | 38,711 | ‥ | ‥ | ‥ | ‥ | ‥ | ‥ | ‥ | ‥ | ‥ | Merson | ‥ | Rocastle (45), Davis (81) | Dixon, Adams, Smith (2) |
| 6 Jan | FA Cup 3rd Rd | Stoke C | A | W 0-1 | 23,827 | ‥ | ‥ | Davis | ‥ | ‥ | ‥ | ‥ | Quinn | ‥ | ‥ | ‥ | Jonsson (76), Rocastle (84) | Quinn |
| 13 Jan | Football League | Wimbledon | A | L 1-0 | 13,793 | ‥ | ‥ | Winterburn | Davis | ‥ | ‥ | ‥ | Smith | ‥ | ‥ | ‥ | Caesar (33), Rocastle (79) | |
| 20 Jan | Football League | Tottenham H | H | W 1-0 | 46,132 | ‥ | ‥ | Davis | Thomas | ‥ | ‥ | Rocastle | ‥ | ‥ | ‥ | Groves | Thomas (74), Merson (84) | Adams |
| 27 Jan | FA Cup 4th Rd | QPR | H | D 0-0 | 43,483 | ‥ | ‥ | Winterburn | Davis | ‥ | ‥ | ‥ | ‥ | ‥ | ‥ | ‥ | Merson (72) | |
| 31 Jan | FA Cup 4th Rd Rp | QPR | A | L 2-0 | 21,547 | ‥ | ‥ | ‥ | ‥ | ‥ | ‥ | ‥ | ‥ | ‥ | ‥ | Merson | Campbell (72) | |
| 17 Feb | Football League | Sheffield W | A | L 1-0 | 20,640 | ‥ | ‥ | Pates | Davis | ‥ | ‥ | ‥ | ‥ | ‥ | ‥ | ‥ | | |
| 27 Feb | Football League | Charlton A | A | D 0-0 | 17,504 | ‥ | ‥ | Winterburn | Thomas | Bould | ‥ | ‥ | ‥ | ‥ | Merson | Marwood | Campbell (84), O'Leary (78) | |
| 3 Mar | Football League | QPR | A | L 2-0 | 18,067 | ‥ | ‥ | ‥ | ‥ | ‥ | ‥ | ‥ | ‥ | ‥ | ‥ | Groves | Campbell (78) | |
| 7 Mar | Football League | Nottingham F | H | W 3-0 | 31,879 | ‥ | ‥ | Winterburn | Thomas | ‥ | ‥ | ‥ | ‥ | ‥ | ‥ | ‥ | Campbell (26), O'Leary (H/T) | Adams, Groves, Campbell |
| 10 Mar | Football League | Manchester C | A | D 1-1 | 29,087 | ‥ | ‥ | ‥ | ‥ | ‥ | ‥ | ‥ | ‥ | ‥ | Campbell | Marwood | Hayes (69) | Marwood |
| 17 Mar | Football League | Chelsea | H | L 0-1 | 33,805 | ‥ | ‥ | ‥ | ‥ | ‥ | ‥ | Hayes | ‥ | ‥ | ‥ | Groves | Hayes (67), O'Leary (81) | |
| 24 Mar | Football League | Derby Co | A | W 1-3 | 17,514 | ‥ | ‥ | ‥ | ‥ | ‥ | ‥ | ‥ | ‥ | ‥ | ‥ | ‥ | O'Leary (83), Ampadu (86) | Hayes (2), Campbell |
| 31 Mar | Football League | Everton | H | W 1-0 | 35,223 | ‥ | ‥ | ‥ | ‥ | ‥ | ‥ | ‥ | ‥ | ‥ | ‥ | ‥ | O'Leary (81), Ampadu (85) | Smith |
| 11 Apr | Football League | Aston Villa | H | L 0-1 | 30,060 | ‥ | ‥ | ‥ | ‥ | ‥ | ‥ | ‥ | O'Leary | ‥ | ‥ | ‥ | Merson (75) | |
| 14 Apr | Football League | Crystal Palace | A | D 1-1 | 28,094 | ‥ | ‥ | ‥ | ‥ | ‥ | ‥ | Davis | ‥ | ‥ | Merson | ‥ | Merson (73), Davis (85) | Hayes |
| 18 Apr | Football League | Liverpool | H | D 1-1 | 33,395 | ‥ | ‥ | ‥ | ‥ | ‥ | ‥ | ‥ | ‥ | ‥ | ‥ | ‥ | Campbell (24), Pates (89) | Merson |
| 21 Apr | Football League | Luton T | A | L 2-0 | 11,595 | ‥ | ‥ | ‥ | ‥ | ‥ | ‥ | Rocastle | ‥ | ‥ | Campbell | ‥ | Hayes (68), Rocastle (68) | |
| 28 Apr | Football League | Millwall | H | W 2-0 | 25,607 | ‥ | ‥ | ‥ | ‥ | ‥ | ‥ | ‥ | Davis | ‥ | Campbell | Marwood | Campbell (74), Marwood | Davis, Merson |
| 2 May | Football League | Southampton | H | W 2-1 | 23,732 | ‥ | ‥ | ‥ | ‥ | ‥ | ‥ | Richardson | ‥ | ‥ | Campbell | ‥ | Richardson (76) | Dixon, Rocastle |
| 5 May | Football League | Norwich C | A | D 2-2 | 19,256 | ‥ | ‥ | ‥ | Hayes | ‥ | ‥ | Rocastle | ‥ | ‥ | Campbell | Groves | O'Leary (59), Groves (59), Thomas (65) | Smith (2) |

Rd Round  Rp Replay  H Home  A Away  WS Wembley Stadium  M Miami  G Glasgow

Compiled by John Burt